EAGLES IN TALL STEEPLES

*Insights into Pastors
and the People They Pastor*

EAGLES IN TALL STEEPLES

CAROLYN WEESE
Foreword by Lloyd John Ogilvie

A Division of Thomas Nelson Publishers
Nashville

Copyright © 1991 by Carolyn Weese

Published in Nashville, Tennessee, by Oliver-Nelson Books, a division of Thomas Nelson, Inc., Publishers, and distributed in Canada by Lawson Falle, Ltd., Cambridge, Ontario.

The Bible version used in this publication is THE NEW KING JAMES VERSION. Copyright © 1979, 1980, 1982, Thomas Nelson, Inc., Publishers.

Printed in the United States of America.

Library of Congress Cataloging-in-Publication Data

Weese, Carolyn, 1938–
    Eagles in tall steeples : insights into pastors and the people
they pastor / Carolyn Weese.
        p.   cm.
    ISBN 0-8407-9123-2
    1. Clergy—Office. 2. Pastoral theology. 3. Weese, Carolyn,
1938–   . 4. Church consultation—United States. I. Title.
BV660.2.W398   1991
253ʹ.2—dc20   90–28124
                                                                      CIP

1 2 3 4 5 6 — 96 95 94 93 92 91

To
my loving husband
Harvey

and to
our daughter and her husband
Karen and Jim O'Neil

They are God's greatest gifts to me.

CONTENTS

FOREWORD

There's a fresh wind blowing. It's blowing away the clouds of cynicism about contemporary Christianity and criticism of the church. This could be one of the finest hours for the church in America. We are on the edge of a great spiritual awakening.

People outside the church are expressing an amazing combination of openness and spiritual hunger. Inside the church there is a restlessness for renewal. Church members are tired of business as usual. They join their voices with secular Americans in calling for dynamic preaching of Christ, for a local church alive with fresh joy and power, and for answers for their deepest needs and most urgent questions.

The greatest concern is that pastors and church officers may not be ready to respond to this propitious time. The church today longs for pastors who are breaking new ground in their own spiritual lives and can call their congregations on to new steps in the adventure of discipleship. As never before, there is a desire for incisive "thus says the Lord," authoritative biblical preaching that comes flaming and burning out of the hearts and minds of preachers. People are ready for their pastors to lead them in a movement rather than simply maintain a religious institution.

Many pastors, particularly of larger churches, often find that they are so bogged down by the demands of a busy ministry and the exhausting challenges of keeping the machinery of the organization oiled that there is little time or energy left to nurture their first love for Christ or to be courageous spiritual leaders of their congregations. The seduction of the secondary sucks them into a pressured life. Problems of staff, the administration of large programs, and the ever-present crises of people depower the eagles of tall steeples.

Some of these eagles have had the courage and maturity to take time to enter into a creative process of evaluating their lives and ministries, to set new goals for themselves and their churches, and to find more effective ways to maximize their administration of the church for mission.

Carolyn Weese, the author of this book, has enabled many of these eagles to soar. They have utilized her services as a consultant in renewal and effective church organization and management. The encouraging stories of what happened to them and their churches is the thrust of this book.

This book is on time and on target for leaders of churches who want to be fully prepared for the awakening God is initiating in our time. It is personal and practical. Here's a book chuck full of insight and inspiration. It should be read by every pastor and church officer who wants to lead his or her church to full potential.

I have known Carolyn Weese for many years as an active, enthusiastic lay leader and then as a creative member of our church staff charged with responsibility for implementing program. Now her years of serving as a consultant to churches has broadened her experience to be a sensitive counselor to leaders and an incisive analyst of a church's needs, as well as the instigator of vision for the most expeditious ways for a church to function with maximum efficiency and effectiveness.

It is a pleasure to commend this book to you with enthusiasm.

LLOYD OGILVIE

INTRODUCTION

You really ought to write a book about your insights into pastors and congregations. It would be a tremendous guide in helping us to understand one another." That comment has been made to me over and over again by pastors and laypeople, during the past five years. Each time that I have heard it, I have received it as a word from the Lord.

How do you write a book that will honestly communicate what makes a pastor tick? How do you describe ministry and the work of the church to laypeople so that they will understand and relate to what is being said? How do you tell this story in general terms when every church is as different as every family living in Big City or Small Town, USA? So dramatically different, but so incredibly similar!!

Eagles in Tall Steeples is written with the hope that pastor and parishioner will see themselves throughout the pages and gain a clearer understanding of one another.

It is my hope to communicate the true heart of a pastor, what makes him or her tick: the torment of discouragement, the frustration of disorganization, the agony of dissension, the joy of serving the Lord, the delight of seeing others grow in their faith, and the fulfillment of his or her vision for ministry. Some may read this and say that I am too partial or sympathetic to clergy. I believe I have been honest, fair, and objective, and I ask the reader to read it in the way it was written. Those who are disillusioned, disappointed, or burned out in the church may perceive this book differently.

This book is not intended to provide answers to all who read it, but instead it will offer insight into many situations found in the church. There are no pat answers for these challenges, but when we can view things objectively and prayerfully the answers come.

In order to get a true perspective of the pastoral role, it is also necessary to look at the congregation, for pastor and people are directly connected. Each chapter, then, will look at a different facet that makes up the church.

The wisdom shared in *Eagles in Tall Steeples* has come from my active involvement in the church for more than thirty years. I was a volunteer serving on committees and participating in the organizations of the church, then a part-time employee, and finally a full-time layperson on the program staff of one of the largest churches in America. After ten years as a staff member, I obeyed the still small voice of God telling me that I had said and done all I could say and do. And I resigned my position.

Having taken that step, the Lord developed within me and opened the doors for a consulting ministry. There the adventure began. "See, I have set before you an open door, and no one can shut it" (Rev. 3:8). Combining the many years of on-the-job training in the church and "pew-gained theology," I walked through the doors as the Lord opened them to me. Consequently, He has taken me into many churches—small and large, urban and suburban, healthy and hurting. He has given me entry into the hearts of pastors, their staff, their leaders, and their congregations. He has allowed me to walk with them in ministry, to help them discover creative ways of being more effective in their call.

It has been a joy to witness the love of Jesus Christ melt denominational barriers, thaw the icy hearts of many church leaders, and energize those who have grown weary in the work of the church. Often I am in awe as I watch the power of the Holy Spirit move in and make peace out of chaos.

The Lord has allowed me to see the church as it really is and has given me a deeper love for it than ever before. It is my hope that this book will communicate at least a small portion of the insight gained as I have sought to share my expertise and the love of Jesus Christ with the local church.

Though the pastoral ministry is dominated by men, I have worked with many women who fill this role as well. I have written a chapter about women in ministry, not to separate them, but to include them and the special gifts and insight that come through women in ministry. Throughout the book, however, pastors are usually referred to as male to make the text more readable.

Special thanks to all of the pastors with whom I have shared in ministry, and especially to those who have pastored, counseled, taught, nurtured, encouraged, and affirmed me in order that this manuscript might be written. God bless each of you.

My deep appreciation to the Rev. David McKechnie, who was relentless in pressing me to get on with the writing; to Mrs. Linda Coleman for working with me in Glen Eyrie, Colorado, as I labored to put the book on tape; and to my daughter, Karen, and her husband Jim, for their encouragement and computer support.

I can never completely express my gratitude to my wonderful husband, Harvey, who saw the vision for this ministry and encouraged me to step out in faith. He gives me the freedom to minister in the name of Christ, provides prayer support as I visit church after church, and strengthens me with his love when I grow weary.

Now, come with me through *Eagles in Tall Steeples* and discover who eagles are, where they are found, and what they are called to do in the sight of God.

CAROLYN WEESE

THE EAGLE

The eagle

Is born an eagle.

Can be found throughout the world.

Comes in many shapes and sizes.

Looks courageous and proud, but is actually a timid hunter.

Has keen eyesight and can see great distances, with a broad perspective; a visionary.

Experiences total freedom, when he catches the wind, and is borne aloft on the wings of the wind which is his natural habitat.

Is set apart. He builds his eyrie at the highest possible point so that he can maintain a perspective.

Claims his own territory, and protects it from other eagles.

Does not flock together with other eagles, but tends to be a loner.

Will sometimes gather with other eagles during the winter where there is an abundance of food.

Seems to know when it is time to die. He will attach his talons to a rock, always a rock, face into the setting sun, and die.

"But they that wait upon the Lord shall renew their strength; they shall mount up with wings as eagles; they shall run, and not be weary; and they shall walk, and not faint" (Isa. 40:31).

CHAPTER 1

EAGLES IN TALL STEEPLES

"And He Himself gave some to be apostles, some prophets, some evangelists, and some pastors and teachers, for the equipping of the saints for the work of ministry, for the edifying of the body of Christ, till we all come to the unity of the faith and the knowledge of the Son of God, to a perfect man, to the measure of the stature of the fullness of Christ."

—Ephesians 4:11–13

How will I recognize you when you get off the plane?"

"Don't worry, I'll know you," I said confidently over the phone. "All of you pastors look alike!"

"Is that so?" the pastor replied. "I'll see you tomorrow," and hung up the phone.

It was my first trip to Texas, and I was looking forward to it. The pastor and I had talked a number of times during the eight months prior to my visit. We had begun to build a good relationship. I walked through the jetway at Houston's Hobby Airport and quickly scanned the waiting area for my "typical pastor." It didn't take long to see that none fit the role.

"Well," I thought, "maybe he is out at the security check point," and started out of the waiting area. I looked carefully at each person I came upon, but none fit "the type."

Standing at the edge of the waiting area leaning on a newspaper rack was what I perceived to be a "typical" Texas cowboy. He wore a ten-gallon hat pulled down on his forehead, sunglasses, western shirt, grubby jeans, and cowboy boots. I looked him up and down and wondered if this could possibly be the pastor I had come to visit. If I spoke to him and he wasn't who I thought, I could be in deep trouble. Picking up a cowboy in an airport was not on my agenda. I decided to do the safe thing and pass him by. As I did, I heard a familiar voice say, "Carolyn?"

That was my introduction to Texas, and since that day I have never claimed that all pastors look alike.

Some pastors may wear rumpled pants, have dandruff on their jacket, wear glasses, and drive conservative grey four-door cars that go no faster than 55 m.p.h. Some, but not all.

Many are meticulous about their appearance and dress fashionably. One afternoon I was packing my bag for a trip and my daughter was providing her usual critique on my travel wardrobe. "Karen," I asked, "you have talked to this pastor several times on the phone. What do you think he looks like?"

She thought a moment, and said, "I think he is about five-foot-ten, has grayish hair, wears pin-striped suits, Oxford cloth button-down-collared shirts, and loafers, and probably uses half-glasses to read."

"Well, that's a pretty complete description. How did you come up with all of that?"

"It's easy, Mom. He just sounds like that."

I confess I walked off the plane looking for one that fit that description, but I was met by the pastor's wife instead. He had had a crisis call at the last minute and had sent his wife to the airport. He would meet us at the restaurant.

At the restaurant, I watched everyone who came through the door. Finally, a man about five-foot-ten with grayish hair who was wearing a pin-striped suit, Oxford cloth button-down-collared shirt, and loafers came through the door. I knew immediately who it was. He introduced himself to me and we went into the restaurant for dinner. As I opened the menu, my friend was taking out his half-glasses to read the bill of fare. My daughter had described him perfectly.

Pastors may be male or female, tall or short, fat or thin, bald or bushy, young or old. They may be neatniks or slobs, extroverts or introverts, but all have the same thing in common—Sunday morning.

Tacked on the robing room door leading to the chancel of one church is a well-worn card stating, THROW THE ARMS OF YOUR HEART AROUND THE CONGREGATION. These are the last words the pastor sees as he steps onto the chancel and leads the congregation in worshiping God. Sunday after Sunday, pastors in churches of all sizes, shapes, and denominations attempt to throw their arms around the church family in an effort to draw them closer to God.

The worship service has been carefully designed to

glorify God and make the hearts of the congregation receptive to the word of the Lord. Hymns are carefully selected; anthems rehearsed; prayers prayed; the Scripture read with dignity; and the sermon delivered with power.

Every Sunday morning the pastor is expected to be upbeat, victorious, and enthusiastic and to preach a more powerful sermon than the week before. It matters not what kind of week the pastor has had. After all, aren't pastors perfect? They have divine protection from career tensions, family crises, personal struggles, and worry. They don't face the everyday hassles that other people face. What do pastors do all week, besides preach a twenty-minute sermon on Sunday morning?

The Reverend Canon Geoffrey Gray wrote, "People expect their priest to have the skill in sermon preparation of Knox, the oratorical power of Churchill, the personal charm of a film star, the tact of royalty, the hide of a hippo, the administrative ability of Lord Nuffield, the wisdom of Socrates, and the patience of Job. Some people must often be disappointed."

When a person responds to the call of God and enters pastoral ministry, their life is set apart. A pastor is set apart to study the Word of God and then to preach and teach it to the congregation. A pastor is set apart from the events of the marketplace, because it is thought he simply cannot relate. A pastor and his family are often set apart, as being something other than the norm; they are often not included in informal get-togethers because they are considered "different." And so, a great portion of ministry time is spent breaking down the barriers that have "set him apart."

The "tall steeple" church (that is, a large congregation with a strong, positive reputation) usually has a senior pastor, or head of staff, who is spiritually mature, with considerable experience in pastoring a congregation of some size. He is a visionary and is highly energetic. Underneath that layer of polish, vision, energy, and charismatic good looks, there is a "Type A" personality. Type A people are normally workaholics who are capable of thinking about and doing several things simultaneously. They often have a great sense of humor, like my cowboy friend, and can laugh at themselves in many instances. They are adventuresome (motorcyclists and mountain climbers), fiercely competitive (play golf, tennis, or racquet ball with them and find out), easily irritated by delays (my flights are frequently late), desire accuracy (a typo in the bulletin), are driven to succeed (they want bigger and better), are outwardly confident (assertive in every way) and inwardly insecure (a pussycat with fears), and they strive to please everyone.

Visionaries can envision more ministry and programs than there are people to fill those ministries and programs. Visionaries tend to get so far out in front of their people that the people often mistake them for the enemy. Visionaries are willing to take risks. When they do take risks, they leave themselves vulnerable to be misunderstood, criticized, or undercut by members of their staff, leadership, or congregation.

Visionaries like to dream the dream and get people pumped to move forward. They prefer to let others capture the dream on paper; they do not like to get bogged down in detail. While staff and committees are trying to figure out how to implement the vision, the visionary is on to a new dream.

Contained within many of these pastors is an entrepreneurial spirit that enjoys being on the cutting edge for new ideas. They are never content with status quo, and they look to the corporate world and high-tech society for ideas that will help them in the continual growth of their church. If they had not followed God's call into ministry, many of these men would be found heading up corporations, developing new marketing strategies, or driving ahead in uncharted territories. At their fingertips are all the high-tech toys—fax machines, car phones, computers, beepers, pocket dictating equipment, etc. They enjoy many of the perks of success: first-class travel, vacation hideaways, new cars, theater tickets, and nice clothes, more often at the generosity of some of their parishioners than at their own expense. They are the first ones to counsel people to "take time to smell the roses," and yet, they cannot relax without feeling guilty.

Tempering these characteristics, the Lord usually blesses the pastor with a high level of sensitivity, compassion, care, and discernment toward those who suffer. Daily he invests himself in the life of his parishioners, hurting where they hurt, walking with them through crisis and grief, giving of himself sacrificially that others might know the love of Jesus Christ in their lives.

They give the appearance that they have it "all together," and often they don't. In the very large churches the senior pastor is expected to be a good pulpiteer. (A *pulpiteer* is one who has studied his text in depth, develops a stimulating message from it, submerges himself in it, and delivers it with power and authority.) Week after week he waxes eloquent from the pulpit. He is energized by his preaching, and considers it to be his strongest gift. These pastors have many of the same dynamics and characteristics going for them as do our finest actors of stage and screen. When a congregation responds positively, the pastor is stimulated to greater heights. When a congregation snoozes apathetically through a service, he feels he has failed his flock and let them down.

THE LARGER THE CHURCH THE GREATER THE CHALLENGE

When a pastor has served in a large church for a number of years, he has usually weathered a number of storms. Sometimes it is a financial crisis in the church; sometimes it is a staffing problem; sometimes it is a group of people in the congregation who have reacted *against* the pastor rather than *for* the pastor. The pastor takes each problem personally because of his sensitive spirit.

Gossip or rumors will fly through a congregation, often directed at the senior pastor. When the layers of gossip are slowly peeled away, seldom is truth at the center of the story. If the pastor reveals the truth of the situation without breaking any confidences, it appears that no one wants to hear it or accept it. The truth is never as sensational as the gossip, and people will continue to believe the stories they first heard. This is destructive and diminishes the credibility of the pastor. The pastor internalizes all this and can be deeply shaken by it. He must work hard to reestablish his credibility and rebuild trust levels in his congregation before he can move forward again.

Staff problems are among the greatest challenges for the head of staff, regardless of the size of the church. In a church where the staff is quite large, turnover occurs on a fairly regular basis. In some churches, it seems there is always a member or members of staff coming or going, and the staffing model seldom remains stable.

When a member of the pastoral staff leaves and goes on to a church of his own or into another area of ministry, rather than seeing that as launching another bright young person into further ministry, a senior pastor often will feel rejected. Deep inside a little voice tells him repeatedly, "You've lost another good person. How could they do this to you? It must be something you've done, to cause them to leave." This is very painful, and it is difficult for the pastor to accept that members of staff will leave under good circumstances. Then, of course, he is faced with redesigning the staff to maintain the present level of effectiveness, and he must begin the search for a new person to join the team.

THE OLD SCHOOL VS. THE NEW SCHOOL

In many instances, the pastors of big churches have served and developed ministries in several churches and in one particular church over a period of years. As seasoned pastors they will often call younger men and women who have very little ministry experience. The difference in their ages may not pose a problem, but the difference in leadership styles can be divisive. The commitment to ministry that the head of staff has known all the years of his ministry is often quite different from the commitment to ministry that the younger men and women have coming out of school today.

Instead of recognizing that they are accountable to the head of staff, many of them believe that they are all equal and resist the direction and the leadership of the head of staff. They resist doing what they are asked to do. They backbite and compete with the head of staff for position. It begins to eat away at the soul of the head of staff until, in many circumstances, he begins to withdraw in his leadership. Instead of being direct and in touch with all of what is going on in his church, the pastor often retreats or moves into other forms of ministry that take him somewhat away from the local parish. Sometimes he becomes involved on a higher level in the denomination, invests time in community efforts, develops a nationwide ministry, writes books, or pursues other such projects in order to feel fulfilled. In the meantime, to the staff and to the people of the congregation, it looks as though the pastor has taken his hands off leadership, that he lets things slide when they should be brought into order. Committees will run rampant and finally say, "We don't have any support from the pastor."

When it reaches that point, the pastor has lost sight of who he is. The pastor has actually allowed staff and congregation to transform him into what their image of him is. When that happens the level of discouragement can get so high that the pastor will take an early retirement or leave the ministry, will leave that pulpit and go into another form of ministry, or will accept a call to another church.

While this is going on, a growing number of the congregation becomes less and less approving of what is or is not happening in the church. Leaders become frustrated with the pastor's inability to lead. He no longer holds the vision in front of the people. Soon the people move beyond the pastor, and they reach a place where they make it uncomfortable for him to stay.

Sometimes months will pass before the pastor realizes he is no longer providing the leadership expected of him. Trying to regain that leadership role usually is impossible, and he is faced with looking for another church. If he does not actively search for a new call, the leadership may reach a peak of frustration and ask him to leave. This is never a healthy or pleasant time in the life of the church or the congregation.

It is interesting to observe how pastors in very large churches differ in leadership style, in the way they preach, in their theology, and in their personal appearance. Even though they are different, most seem to have a tender, gentle, caring spirit. That spirit can get wounded deeply over a period of years if staff and members of a congregation consistently take critical potshots at them. Each time one of those potshots lands, the resulting wound often causes a pastor to retreat and become someone other than who he really wants to be. By acknowledging this fact, the pastor can understand what is happening to him and can begin the process of self-evaluation, rebuild his confidence, and reestablish his sense of direction. Whether pastors or parishioners, when we face the difficult times, we must come to the place where we "rejoice in the hope of the glory of God. And not only that, but we also glory in tribulations, knowing that tribulation produces perseverance; and perseverance, character; and character, hope. Now hope does not disappoint, because the love of God has been poured out in our hearts by the Holy Spirit who was given to us" (Rom. 5:2–5). *Impatient at persevering; weary of character building; hope comes as surely as the dawn.*

When times get tough in the church, when pastors get pulled in many directions, I encourage them to never lose sight of who they are and what they are called to be. For many years during staff meetings, I looked at a paperweight lying on the coffee table in the pastor's study, and my eyes stared at the words inscribed on it, TO BE AND NOT TO SEEM. That phrase haunted me until I grasped its true meaning.

To be a lover of God,
    Not just another religious man or woman.
        That you might sense His touch, and know His
            complete and abundant love.
To be called and ordained of God,
    Not of man.
        That you will be fulfilled in ministry.
To be God's servant in ministry,
    Not just filling a role.
        That you might be served.
To be a lover of your family,
    Not just a husband or wife and father or mother.
        That you will be greatly loved by them.
To be there for your wife or husband,
    Not too busy ministering elsewhere.
        That you will be cherished by your spouse.
To be the example for your children,
    Not just another influence.
        That they will reflect your ways.
To be a lover of your congregation,
    Not just a preacher.
        That they will love others.
To be one who takes time to care,
    Not just to counsel.
        That others will take time to care.
To be a faithful student of God's Word,
    Not just a token scholar.
        That your students will also be fed.

To be a lover of the less fortunate,
   Not just the successful.
      That as you love even these,
      You will love God completely and abundantly.
To be humble,
   And walk with God.
      That is to be . . . and not to seem.

CHAPTER 2

EAGLES IN SMALL STEEPLES

"If I cannot do great things, I can do small things in a great way."

The pastor, sipping lemonade in the warm afternoon sun, sat on the little porch of the home of an aging parishioner. They talked for a long time about the loneliness she felt after her husband died. They discussed the little church of which they were a part and of the many ways God was blessing the lives of its members. An hour or two passed, and the pastor prayed with his friend, gave her a reassuring pat on the hand, and was on his way. He stopped by the insurance office, where he works to subsidize his income, to tend to some business. Then, on his way home, he made a hospital visit to a happy mother and her new baby and a call to the nearby convalescent home to pray for one whose life was slipping away. This is a glimpse of pastoral ministry in a small congregation in a small community. However, pastoring a small flock is more than assurance and insurance.

How does ministry in the small church differ from that in the large church? The call of God to pastoral ministry is as profound to pastors serving the tiniest of congregations as it is to those serving the largest.

Ministry is never easy, and ministry in the small church is no exception. It has been said that approximately 95 percent of the people who enter pastoral ministry will never become a head of staff. They will spend their careers ministering in small parishes, yoked fields or circuit settings (two or more congregations who share the leadership of one pastor), or become associate pastors in larger churches.

Stress, frustration, and anxiety are found in the small church pastor just as it is in the large. Just as I have heard discouraged pastors of large churches moan about the problems and say they want to serve quiet, little country churches with one hundred members, so I have heard pastors of small churches long to be in big churches so they could be free of the difficulties they face. The old theory of the grass looking greener on the other side of the fence definitely applies in ministry.

ALL IN THE FAMILY

Thousands of pastors are serving parishes that cannot financially support them and are otherwise employed. Many of them work in the fields of accounting, sales, counseling, and insurance (like the pastor just mentioned). Their outside income supports them so they can minister to their small flocks. In many instances, larger churches or the denomination will subsidize a pastor so that he can work full-time in ministry.

In the small congregation, ministry becomes personalized. The pastor is viewed as a member of the family; after all, he is the one they call on for weddings, baptisms, funerals, and hospital calls. If he doesn't stop by for a "visit" on a regular basis, the family will inquire about his whereabouts.

Small churches sometimes struggle for growth because they become so cliquish they don't readily welcome new people in the congregation. If the pastor encourages new members, the old members may be very upset with him. Content with who they are, they resist anything that looks like change. The church family often becomes possessive and controlling of a pastor and his ministry. They feel that if they are putting something in the offering plate, they have permission to tell the pastor when and how to do ministry. The pastor becomes owned by the congregation to the extent that he may feel little freedom to build ministry according to God's leading; instead, he capitulates to the wishes of the congregation. Members of the congregation will watch how the pastor spends his money and question even the most trivial things, such as why the pastor should desire a new, colorful phone in the manse, when the old black one has done just fine for twenty-five years.

Some of the most successful ministries in smaller churches have come from women. Once she is accepted by the congregation, a woman is often able to develop ministry to a greater extent than a man filling the same position. The small church concept may be more conducive for women than for men. Women may not be as intimidating or aggressive as some men, and they are more warmly received. Women are often better listeners, and the church family wants to be listened to. And women are excellent at organizing, getting people involved, and building a community feeling. A successful ministry in a small church cannot be measured in the same way that it is measured in the larger church. Ministry in a small church is measured by the depth of the pastor's personal involvement, one-to-one availability, compassion, and care, as well as his teaching and preaching abilities. If he managed to clear a parking lot or build a building, that is quite nice; but the true measure of his ministry is in how he conducted Aunt Bessie's funeral, and the fact that he stayed with the family until the last person went home.

CULTIVATING GROWTH

There are numerous small churches that grow into large churches, and the ministry there is quite different. A small congregation that is open to receiving new members and wants to grow encourages and supports the pastor in his evangelistic efforts. They want him to call on the unchurched. In fact, if the congregation is really excited about their faith and what is happening at the church, they will call on the unchurched with the pastor. As new members are added, the old-timers receive them graciously. The pastor is stimulated to new heights by this response and works harder at developing programs to meet the needs of his growing congregation.

Though in the early stages the pastor may be the only paid employee, he is still serving a multistaff church. That multistaff may include all the roles he is trying to fill, as well as the key lay leaders who are filling roles that eventually could become paid positions. A small church of this type does not stay small for long; staff is soon added, and buildings are built to accommodate the growth. Two important dynamics are at work in this situation. First, the pastor is a man of great potential, ability, energy, and know-how. Second, the congregation is alive, enthusiastic, unafraid of change, and ready to follow the leading of the pastor.

DIFFERENT STYLES FOR DIFFERENT SIZES

The world tends to measure success by "bigger" and "better." If a pastor has done a great job pastoring a church of one hundred people, the obvious thinking is he would do an even better job at pastoring three hundred. Or, if he's developed a church to three hundred, he ought to be able to take one with six hundred members and develop it to one thousand. In reality it does not always work that way. Ministry at different levels requires a different style. Unless a pastor has unlimited vision and energy and is extremely creative, it could be and often is disastrous to climb the numbers ladder in the church.

A pastor may be relatively successful in a small setting, only to struggle and fail in a larger parish. The size of the church is not the only factor in why pastors fail; the locale also can be important. Moving from one section of the country to another, from a country setting to an urban one, or from the inner city to the suburbs means a change in lifestyle and way of thinking. If the pastor does not quickly adjust to these changes, he will find resistance at almost every turn.

When a pastor moves from a small setting to a significantly larger one, he finds that the basic core of a staff is in place to assist in the ministry. No longer is he the center around which everything happens.

Others now share in that effort. Learning how to manage a staff and delegate ministry can be an overwhelming task to the inexperienced pastor. He must be more thorough in his planning and plan more extensively than in the smaller setting. Also he now has a staff that must be motivated to plan. And he must interweave his staff's plans with his. He has to meet deadlines in order for others to do their work adequately. He finds that administering the church takes more time than he thought, especially if he is not a good administrator, and the days of sipping lemonade on someone's porch grow fewer and fewer. The congregation wants pastoral contact, however, and he doesn't know how to do that along with everything else.

After two or three years at this pace, he finds he can't keep up and the quality of ministry is just not there. The congregation becomes unhappy, and he moves on to another church, where it could happen to him again. The solution to all this is to work hard and smart by managing time well. If a pastor is of average ability, he will do well in the smaller settings. *The larger the church, the greater the demands for higher than average ability and energy.* In the marketplace it is common to see people promoted beyond their competence. The same is true in the church, and it happens at every level of size.

STUCK IN THE RUT

The room was filled with about twenty-five pastors, men and women of all ages and in all stages of ministry. They were all of the same denomination from the same geographical region, and, except for a few, they were all pastoring small churches. My first impression was, "What a sorry looking group of folks."

As I listened to them, my impression did not change a great deal. They were the most lackluster, burned-out, dried-up group of clergy I had ever seen. One of the first questions they asked was, "We don't understand why our churches aren't growing. Can you help us?"

I could understand why the churches weren't growing, but I wasn't sure I could be of much help. We talked for many hours, and they shared how they had had ministry sucked out of them by their congregations. They said that at times they felt as though they were being devoured. Some talked about the difficulty in getting people to help with ministry, others talked about conflicts within the congregation. A week away for rest and study was a rare thing, as there was no one available to cover for them in case of an emergency. We talked about their spiritual life, and I quickly discovered that it had dried up as the ministry dried up. It was no wonder that they were having such problems. I wish they could have seen themselves, a bedraggled band—they would have understood immediately why they were experiencing difficulties.

It was interesting to watch one young man who was working in new church development share his enthusiasm and love for his work. As he talked, the others couldn't stand it and fired negative comments until he gave up and was quiet.

This group had become the "plodders" of ministry. A group of "this is the way we've always done it, so this is the way it will continue to be done" people. They had become discouraged in their role and didn't know how to get out of it, and some may not have had the energy to get out of it. They had been getting by on the same ministry that they produced year in and year out. The big question to ask in this situation is, did the pastor turn the congregation into a stagnant pond that initiated the drying-up process? Or was it the congregation, so set in their ways, that turned the pastor into a plodder and killed his dream for ministry? I believe both of these dynamics are at work in almost every instance.

Small steeple churches are prevalent in the inner city. Once flourishing bastions of the faith, perhaps with the tall steeple image of days gone by, now struggling with a different culture and environment. Maintenance of a decaying structure soaks up budget dollars that could be spent to build staff or program to bring this church back to life again. Ministry in these churches has become the helping hand of the community, with soup kitchens, clothes closets, shelters, and the like. Pastors called to this form of ministry are doing a great work and are seldom recognized.

We also see in the inner city congregations that have diminished to only a handful. In actuality, it is time to close the doors and merge two or even three congregations so that health might come back into the body again. But the emotions of the faithful remnant ride high, and they would rather struggle with only a handful than expand the church family in order to be ministered to more completely. When this situation exists under a denomination's umbrella, it is often difficult to make such a move, but in time healing and wholeness comes. Finding people with the courage to recognize the need and facilitate that blending of congregations is almost impossible.

There is a tendency among pastors of small churches to feel as though they are in ministry all by themselves. They think that the problems they are encountering are limited to their situation. Seldom do they look around, connect with other clergy, and learn that they are all in the same situation together. The loneliness of ministry engulfs many good pastors and destroys those who do not have the inner drive and persistence to stick with a situation and improve it.

One group of pastors from struggling inner city churches told me that they would like an expert to come in and tell them how to build ministry in the inner city. They failed to recognize that the experts were in that room. They didn't need another expert— they needed someone who would facilitate a discussion to bring forth the creative ideas, energy, and a plan that would improve the situation in their area.

THE SWEETNESS OF MINISTRY

The sweetness of ministry in small congregations is evident when a pastor knows not just every *name*, but every *person*. He has the opportunity to lead people to Christ and disciple them into spiritual maturity. He watches families blend and shares their joys and their sorrows with them. He knows fulfillment when his preaching and teaching are well received, and his congregation responds to it. He becomes a respected leader of a small community and may umpire at Little League games, serve on the school board, or work in other ways for the betterment of the community. True success comes when the pastor knows beyond a shadow of a doubt that he is where God would have him be, and that brings a great sense of freedom. He aspires to no more than this, and his heart soars for God as he reaches out to his flock.

"Jesus said to him, 'Feed my sheep'" (John 21:17).

CHAPTER 3

WALKING THE WALK

"As the deer pants for the water brooks, so pants my soul for you, O God. My soul thirsts for God, for the living God."

—Psalm 42:1–2

From the time we come to Christ we are taught, preached to, and encouraged to build our own spiritual life. Many of us have guilt trips laid on us for not having a consistent quiet time. If we don't do that at some hour like 5:00 A.M., we are less than all that God wants us to be. And so we make fledgling attempts at building a spiritual life, having a quiet time, or having morning devotions. That is met with varying degrees of success, depending on our stages in life. It is no different for pastors.

COME APART OR COME APART!

I believe that pastors often preach sermons they need most to hear themselves. When we hear pounding forth from the pulpit the need for all of us to build our inner life, to spend more time in study and prayer, to truly walk with God, that is usually the time the preacher has realized that he has drifted away from it.

Pastors write a weekly sermon and spend a lot of time doing research. They study portions of Scripture in depth, refer to the Greek or Hebrew, and consult commentaries. That is not the same as feeding on the Scripture for their own personal growth and developing a time to be still before the Lord and to commune with Him through prayer. Eventually a pastor may question why he doesn't have fresh ideas to bring to his people through his sermons, and he fails to see that he is not being fed.

I have seen a pastor in a time of crisis, and the only thing that kept him putting one foot in front of the other was the fact that he disciplined himself to walk with God daily.

I spent a week at Mickey's church helping the staff develop better organizational techniques. Throughout the week, Mickey and I spent a great deal of time working over position descriptions for the staff, revamping committee structure and responsibilities, and evaluating programs with the thought that linking all of this together would build effective communication and maximize the effort of paid staff and lay leadership.

Daily we spent time together praying through the process, seeking God's direction in our work. At one point in my visit, I asked him how he builds his spiritual life. He smiled, and said, "That's easy to describe. I get up about 4:30 or 5:00 A.M., go out to my chair in the living room, read the Scriptures, and pray. I read devotional books as well as other good Christian books. Sometimes I sing hymns or sing psalms unto

God. I praise the Lord during this time, and I listen for what He would have me know that day." He went on to tell me that he spends sixty to ninety minutes in devotions with the Lord each day, and for the last twenty-five years he has read the Scriptures in their entirety four times each year.

My first thought to all of this was, "what great discipline." But, as he explained, what started out as a regimented discipline grew into hours of enjoyment. He counts that early morning time as treasured moments with a best friend.

That evening when we arrived at his home, I peeked into the living room and quickly recognized a comfortable, well-worn chair with a table holding a well-used Bible, books, pads of paper, and pens, and I knew immediately that I had found the place where he spends time with the Lord each day.

About a year after my visit to Mickey's church, a time of crisis struck the church. Through those difficult months Mickey was sustained by the wellspring deep within him. I believe if it had not been for the depth of his spiritual life, he would not have been able to make the decisions he made, or think or act as God's man in that place to bring resolution to the challenges he faced.

By driving the wellspring deep, "panting at the water's edge," drinking from the Water of Life, pastors have been strengthened and carried over the toughest of times that they face in ministry. The pastors that don't have this wellspring in their inner being struggle with many things. When a challenge comes, be it a financial crisis in the church, staff conflict, or personal difficulty, they have so little to draw from that they often go down in defeat. *All of who we are inwardly will determine all of what we are outwardly!*

In the sixteenth century a great thinker, Hugo Grotius, had this to say:

> He knows not how to rule a kingdom, that cannot manage a province; nor can he wield a province, that cannot order a city; nor he order a city, that knows not how to regulate a village, nor he a village that cannot guide a family; nor can that man govern well a family that knows not how to govern himself, neither can any govern himself unless his Reason be Lord . . .
> Nor can Reason rule unless herself be ruled, by God, and wholly be obedient to Him.

The issue today is not theology, but spirituality. Our pastors are well schooled, often with advanced degrees. They think in scholarly terms, and they are often stimulated by great discussions over theological matters. Theology feeds the intellect, but spirituality shapes the heart and nourishes the soul.

Picture a beautiful banquet table set with fine linen and silver. The flowers have been arranged, the candles lit, and the finest food is on the table. The only guest is seated and begins to enjoy the food and the fellowship of the host. The butler is busy overseeing the scene, listening to bits and pieces of the conversations. In the kitchen, he nibbles on the crumbs that have been left behind from the banquet. He was very present and yet not a participant.

Modern day scholars and theologians are like the butler. They can give us an accurate account of the event; however, they may not have experienced it as a guest. Jesus Christ invites us to be His guest at the banquet. No longer feasting on the leftover crumbs, each individual is the guest invited to a table set for two. There, as he or she draws up a chair to the table, all life takes on new meaning; time stands still as two hearts intertwine. This fellowship is so perfect that we share with Him our fears and failures, our sins and struggles, our temptations and trials, and our joys in knowing Him. And as we do this, "[He] forgives all [our] iniquities . . . heals all [our] diseases, [and] . . . redeems [our] life from destruction," and loves us with a love that will not let us go. He encourages us and strengthens us for what lies ahead.

Spirituality dwells in the heart. Regular attendance at worship, memorizing favorite hymns, taking communion, and providing service in the church are all outward expressions of faith and may meet worldly standards. *When our hearts kneel in His presence, and we open ourselves to Him, Jesus Christ will fill us with Himself, teach us what we need to learn, and lead us to do what He would have us do.*

The church is a living organism, the center of which is the heart. For the church to be a healthy organism, the members of the body must know a personal relationship with Jesus Christ. Anything less than this weakens the organism. *The Christian life is a journey, not a destination, and the journey begins with committing one's life to Christ.* In the church we must never take for granted that everyone has taken that step in life. We must continually provide opportunities for people to come to the saving grace of Jesus Christ.

Christianity is but one generation away from extinction, and so it is for every Christian to be equipped with a vital, growing, reproducible faith. Though it may be the pastor's responsibility to equip us with the faith, it is our responsibility to share that faith and the reason for our joy with those we meet.

"You have something I don't have, and I want it," an elder said to me at the close of a meeting. He made an appointment to see me later in the week. When he arrived his first words to me were, "How can I become a Christian?" I looked into this dear gentleman's eyes and saw the sincerity with which he asked the question. What puzzled me was he was nearly seventy years old and had been an active church member all his life.

He and his wife had given leadership in planting a new church; he had preached on numerous occasions. He had been an elder for thirty-five years, yet he wanted to know how to become a Christian. As I talked with him, it was clear to me that he had never given his life to Christ and that was what he wanted to do that day. It was a beautiful moment when we joined hands to pray and invited Jesus Christ to live in his heart. He left that meeting place a new man.

I stayed in touch with him and he grew steadily in his walk with Christ. No longer interested in buildings, grounds committees, or budgets, he wanted to be in ministry. He became a lay counselor and is reaching out to touch others for Christ.

GETTING STARTED AGAIN

Pastors often talk with me about their search for a way to deepen their spiritual life. When they ask me if I know of seminary classes or workshops that they might attend, I tell them that course credits or a quick-fix workshop do not build spirituality. Instead, spirituality is built through a journey that begins with the heart and not the intellect.

"What must I do to get started again?" they will ask. I tell them that they have already begun. Just by raising the question they have realized that there is a void in their life and that they are hungering for something more. Then I share with them a simple, nine-step plan that helped me in my journey.

1. Take vitamins. Take a good supply of natural vitamins and eat a well-balanced diet. Our lifestyle often is such that we may miss meals or eat on the run. Vitamins replenish what we miss in our diet. Our bodies are temples for the Holy Spirit, and it is important that we take care of ourselves.

2. Exercise. Many major illnesses are brought on by stress. Studies show that Americans suffer more from emotional stress rather than from physical stress. A regular exercise routine will relieve stress and strengthen the physical body.

3. Rest. Adequate rest replenishes our strength for the new day and freshens our outlook on the future.

4. Study. Read the Scripture daily. When pastors ask for help, I share with them the same things they probably share with a new Christian. I suggest they begin by reading the gospels, the psalms, the letters, the books of history and the prophets. Instead of looking for sermon material, I encourage them to feed on the Word until their thirst is quenched. As the hymn says, "Bread of Heaven, feed me till I want no more."

If we can spend a half hour every day pouring over the morning paper, surely we can spend the same amount of time studying the Word of God that contains all the answers to life's questions.

5. Be still. "Be still and know that I am God." Listen for the still, small voice of God. When our hearts are quiet in His presence, He reveals to us His plans for our future. "For I know the thoughts that I think toward you," says the Lord, "thoughts of peace and not of evil, to give you a future and a hope. Then you will call upon Me and go and pray to Me, and I will listen to you. And you will seek Me and find Me when you search for Me with all your heart. I will be found by you" (Jer. 29:11–14). We are so good at rushing into His presence with our requests, then dashing off to do our work—in the Lord's name but with our strength. That is religion. Trusting God, listening to Him, following His lead, and functioning on His power is the key to an abundant life.

6. *Pray.* "The effective, fervent prayer of a righteous man avails much" (James 5:16). We simply do not tap the power source of faith the way we should. We struggle along on our own steam, and we pray to let God know that we are trying our best, rather than allow Him to bring about His best for all of us. There is unlimited power in prayer if we will only grasp it. Many folks, including pastors, feel inadequate when it comes to praying. They have never been taught to pray aloud and are reluctant to do so for fear they will sound childish or inept. All the sermons and books about prayer will never teach us how to pray. The only way is simply to pray. In prayer we draw close to God; the more we pray, the stronger the bond. It is in taking this step that we begin to know the mind of Christ and can apply that in all that we do. My prayer life changed dramatically when I began to pray aloud. I was no longer distracted in my thoughts. I became focused on what I was bringing before the Lord, and in those moments I found He would guide my prayers as I prayed. Prayer truly is sweet communion.

7. *Play music.* Select your favorite music and play it often. Whether it is a great hymn of the church, a

contemporary gospel selection, or one of the classics, play tapes of it while you drive or while you relax at home. Music plays a big role in ministering to the soul. It becomes like the balm of Gilead to soothe the weary spirit. As we draw closer to God, the Holy Spirit moves ever deeper within us. Soon we feel His song in our hearts without listening to outside sources. When we waken in the middle of the night, the words and melody of a favorite hymn or chorus ring in our hearts. As we greet the new day, He gives us another song, and later in our day, another song, and yet more songs into the night. Allow the Spirit to put a song back into your heart.

8. *Read.* Read good Christian books aimed at developing spirituality and building an inner life. By reading about building our spiritual life we gain the inner strength to cope with the challenges of the world. It has been said that the books we read and the people with whom we associate will determine where we will be five years from today. Consider what you have been reading in the past year. Is that the journey you wish to travel?

9. *Record your thoughts.* In the initial stages of this plan, I suggest that a journal be kept to reflect the new things that are being discovered, the new energy, and the new feelings of closeness to Christ. Some people do this for a while and then slack off. Others find it so rewarding that they continue the practice faithfully.

These are nine simple steps for building an inner life, for plumbing the wellspring deep within the soul. *It begins with the heart, for the heart is the lens into our soul.* Once our heart is surrendered to God, He can begin a great work within us. The more we let go of ourselves and allow Him to take control, the more power and energy He gives. That is the abundant life. That is walking the walk.

It may come as a surprise to many laypeople that pastors need to hear these words of counsel. After all, they are in the profession to teach us these things, and they know the steps I have outlined. But with the pressure of ministry, they can and do get pulled away from these disciplines. Being confronted anew, they eagerly move back into the walk with Christ again. Pastor or parishioner, we are all pilgrims on a journey. Each of us needs to be reminded of the importance of being on our knees in complete surrender to our Lord and Savior in our hearts.

I got up early one morning
and rushed right into the
day.
I had so much to accomplish
that I didn't have time to
pray.
Problems just tumbled about
me, and heavier came each
task.
"Why doesn't God help me?" I
wondered. He answered,
"You didn't ask."
I wanted to see joy and beauty,
but the day toiled on, gray
and bleak.
I wondered why God didn't
show me. He said, "But you
didn't seek."
I tried to come into God's
presence: I used all my keys
at the lock.

God gently and lovingly
chided, "My child, you
didn't knock."
I woke up early this morning
and paused before entering
the day;
I had too much to accomplish
that I had to take time to
pray.

CHAPTER 4

PASTORING THE PASTOR

"He is no fool who gives up what he cannot keep, to gain that which he cannot lose."

—Jim Elliot

Peter Drucker, America's guru of management, reports that the toughest job in America is to be the President of the U.S., a president of a major university, a chief administrator of a large hospital, or a senior pastor of a large church. Loneliness is one thing these roles have in common. Though surrounded constantly by advisers, coworkers, and significant others related to the particular occupation, loneliness is ever present. The air gets thin for those who rise to the top of their profession. The pressure to make decisions that are quick and correct fosters a lonely feeling.

A pastor's ordination sets him apart as a minister of the gospel, but because of the office he holds, people also set him apart. A pastor tends to be placed on a pedestal. When this happens, it is difficult for him to get close to people or for people to get close to him. Therefore, it becomes a lonely career. Pastors are in need of being pastored just as every parishioner is in need of pastoring. The questions we need to ask are these: How do you pastor a pastor? and Who can do it?

When I first began a consulting ministry to the local church, I was insecure in who I was and not entirely certain of what God was calling me to do. I had never traveled without my husband, and I was fearful of traveling from city to city, arranging for hotels, renting cars, and so forth. To protect myself, I would suggest to the pastor that to save money he could meet me at the airport, and if there was room I would be willing to stay in his home. *Pastors usually like a bargain!* By doing this, I had someone to take care of me during my time away from home. At the time, I didn't realize that my pending visit usually raised the anxiety level of the pastor and his family from above average to out-of-sight. I'm quite sure that he thought, *A strange woman is coming to look at my church, and now she will invade my private domain, my haven of safety. What if the kids misbehave? What if she doesn't like my wife's cooking? How will we entertain her? We need to paint the spare bedroom!* While he fretted with anxiety, my primary blissful thought was, *I will be safe.* My secondary thought was, *This will give me an opportunity to get acquainted with his wife and family, and perhaps pick up some insights from the pastor in a more relaxed setting.*

I knew that my working days would be twelve to fourteen hours in length and that I would not be underfoot at home, but they didn't know that until we planned the agenda for my time. Upon my arrival I tried to be friendly, warm, unpretentious, and as non-threatening as possible. My goal was to "just be family." Generally, it would not take long before pastor and wife would discover a good listening ear and begin to unfold things they had held very deep within themselves. That's when pastoring the pastor—and usually his family—would begin.

What is the key to building that kind of relationship? Is it just taking an interest in who they are? Is it being empathetic with what they share? Is it being able to tell them that many pastors go through the same thing? What is the key? Trust. I believe it is a special gift from God that pastors trust me as quickly as they do.

Recently I was invited to be a resource person at a pastors' conference. I was not the speaker but a participant, and I was the only woman among forty men. Two hours into the conference a pastor sought me out; within thirty minutes he was unloading a career crisis on me and asking for help in resolving it. That was trust. Why did that happen so quickly? I was willing to invest some time in him, to listen to his story, and to explore with him how to deal with it. I was gentle but direct and honest in what I had to say to him.

Here's another instance. I had arrived in a pastor's home on Saturday afternoon, and he and his family and I had a wonderful evening together getting acquainted. Sunday morning was very full—he preached three services. After we had a delightful lunch, he was about to excuse himself to take his usual Sunday pastoral nap.

As we stood in the kitchen talking, I heard pain in his voice as he commented on his upbringing. I casually asked, "What is your relationship with your father?"

That question was like a rock hitting a mirror. It shattered the facade that had been so carefully patched together out of pain and went right to his inner soul. The expression on his face was one I will never forget. The "I've-got-it-all-together" facade had crumbled, and a very weary man looked at me and said, "Do you really want to hear that story?"

"Only if you would like to share it," I responded. With that permission, the remaining barriers fell, and he allowed me into his life and ministry.

Toward the end of my visit, I asked him what it was that caused him to trust me so quickly. He thought a moment and said, "No one has ever asked me about my father and the way I feel as a result of that relationship. You knew the right questions to ask, and I let you into my life. I knew I could trust you."

Pastoring begins with trust. When a pastor chooses to trust me, he allows me to pastor him. Some pastors have mentors, spiritual directors, counselors, support groups, and clergy associations. Through these contacts, they are pastored to some extent. But there are countless pastors who do not have a support network and are in tremendous need of pastoring.

I have found this is especially true in smaller churches. Since the staff is generally small, the pastor does not have the time—or does not take the time—to build a support network locally. Budgets are limited and the pastor often cannot afford to travel to a support group, seek continuing education at seminary, or attend conferences. In small communities spiritual directors are not readily available. And pastors living in small communities are reluctant to seek counseling because they fear it will get back to their congregation. Even though they believe that every good counselor needs a counselor, it somehow does not apply to their situation.

Pastors call me to their church to analyze and evaluate the organization of the church. They brace themselves to hear that they may not be running things very well, that they need to set aside more money for equipment, staff, program, or that they need to decrease or expand staff. They often need help in staff development, long-range planning, or improved communication among staff, committees, boards, and congregation.

Pastors do not call me to their church to pastor them; and yet in the midst of all the analysis being done, that is what it consistently comes down to. I am often viewed as a nonthreatening, interested, somewhat knowledgeable, nonordained woman, a stranger passing through who understands pastoral ministry. The joy of coming alongside someone to encourage, to inspire, to counsel, and to pray is something that can never be fully described.

HOW TO PASTOR!

What do I do to pastor pastors? I listen to them, to what they are saying, and especially to what they are not saying. An appropriate question at the right place (like the one addressed to my friend in the kitchen) can unlock volumes of unspoken history that they have carried around inside for years. I have no routine, no line of questioning. I take a sincere interest in the person, and the rest happens as a result of that interest. I know that God has given me the gifts and abilities to cut through the surface rather quickly to look deeply into people's lives and circumstances. That's an awesome position in which to be placed, and I quietly pray all through the conversation that the Lord will reveal what needs to be known.

I am an encourager of pastors. I help them to see that things can't be as awful as they think and that there is a way through it. I try to show them that path. Though I may encourage them in their ministry, I don't let them get away with ignoring issues or producing less than quality ministry. I have been accused of being tough on pastors, and that may be true. I also believe in "no pain, no gain," and many pastors have had to face the things that harm their ministry and prevent them from moving forward. Bringing about change in a church is a slow process. Bringing about change in a pastor may be not only slow but painful. Perhaps I hold pastors accountable in a way that others have been unable to do.

It is important to remain objective and not get caught up in the problems that pastors share. There is nothing to gain if two people get bogged down in the struggle. I hold many things in confidence, because they have trusted me and often have shared very personal things. There have been instances where, after evaluating the situation, I have told a pastor it is time for him to retire. On other occasions, I have helped a pastor relocate because it was clear he was no longer effective in his present parish.

I arrived in the Seattle area late one Saturday afternoon and had a brief visit with the pastor. This was one of those rare occasions when I was not staying in his home (his family was large and there was no room). Sunday was a very full day. That evening as the pastor drove me to the place where I was staying I said, "Now, Mark, I really need some significant time with you before we get too far into this week. I have looked over the agenda that you've made out for me, and you have filled the time pretty well. Unless I have a pretty clear idea of who you are and what you are all about in ministry, I will not be a lot of help to you."

We decided that the next night after the last meeting we would go to his office and discuss ministry. Monday was another very full day. By the end of the afternoon I learned that Mark would meet an elder and me for dinner at a restaurant. We enjoyed a delightful dinner and conversation, and as we walked out of the restaurant, Mark explained to the elder that he and I had to attend another meeting that evening, and the elder was soon on his way. When I asked Mark where he was parked, he motioned around the corner from the restaurant.

Around the corner was a boat dock, and the next thing I knew, he was helping me into a large cabin cruiser. This was our only transportation back to his car. He turned the key in the ignition and off we went at high speed. About a mile or so offshore he cut the engine, turned around in his seat, propped his feet up on the backseat, and announced, "We are in my office!"

We bobbed around on that lake for four hours as we talked about ministry. He spilled his heart out and shared the challenges and the crises of the past few years, the hopes and dreams for the future, the mistakes and the victories, the joys and the struggles of ministry, the call of God on a person's life, and how the pastor and the parish can build an inner life. We talked of the wonders of God, and we spent time praying through the things we had discussed. In those hours, we covered a lot of territory because there were no interruptions, we were in a relaxed setting, and he could be real. Those were rich hours for both of us, and those were hours of pastoring a pastor.

Who can pastor a pastor? It can be a friend, a counselor, a colleague, or a "significant other." In the latter instance, a spouse doesn't count, because she or he is too close to the source to be objective enough to help.

Pastoring a pastor is one of those things that just happens. We may make an appointment with a counselor for counseling, but I don't know of anyone who schedules an appointment to be pastored. A member of the congregation may make an appointment with the pastor for counseling, and in that appointment time the pastor not only will counsel, he will pastor the person.

The same is true for the pastor. I never walk into a situation thinking that I am going to pastor the pastor. It is an outfall of the work to which I have been called at that particular church. Timing is important in all of this, and I believe that God's timing is perfect. In every instance, it is clear that the Lord has prepared the way, and that's why it happens the way it does.

Is the same need for pastoring found in associate pastors and other members of staff? The need is definitely there, although the dynamics and concerns may be a bit different. Generally, staff members are not as isolated as the head of staff. They tend to have other staff members or friends in the congregation or community to sound off to and be ministered unto. Associate pastors, assistant pastors, and staff members have one thing in common: They all work for the same head of staff. They are all in it together. In some instances they seek out one another for pastoring; in other situations they may have their own spiritual director, mentor, or significant other. There is no doubt about it—they are as much in need of pastoring as anyone.

If a pastor has not been pastored for a long period of time, he tends to lose his tenderness. He builds up a defensive shell of protection, withdraws, and separates himself from the congregation and staff. He begins to dry up. It is one thing for him to develop a powerful spiritual life, to spend a great amount of time with the Lord in study and prayer, *but there are times when he must have God in the flesh.* That person is often a best friend who genuinely cares for him, pastors him, loves him in spite of his warts, and is tough enough to straighten him out if he is headed in the wrong direction. If he doesn't have God in the flesh to be that pastor to him, then I believe he will eventually become less sensitive to the needs of the people around him.

Pastors can be pastored from a distance. The encouragement and affirmation extended in sincerity at sanctuary doors on Sunday mornings mean a great deal to pastors. But encouragement and affirmation extended at unexpected moments and in times of crisis mean more than anyone will ever know or understand. It's during the difficult times that pastors need at least a few solid people who can encourage them to move forward.

Of all the ways we can pastor a pastor, praying for him is probably the best and the most effective. As members of the flock, we are constantly in the position to be the receiver of the pastor's prayers. We hear him pray for us during the morning service; he visits us in the hospital and prays for us; he counsels us in his office; and he prays with us before we leave. We invite him to our home for dinner and ask him to ask the blessing over the food. *Have you ever wondered if and when the pastor hears someone praying for him?* We may pass by him on Sunday morning, pat him on the back, and say, "We're praying for you, Pastor," but when does he hear someone praying for him by name? I've asked that question to a great many pastors, and most of them say they seldom experience that touch of ministry. One pastor told me it had been years since he had heard someone pray for him.

It was early in my consulting work that I discovered this pattern. I now make it a practice when possible to pray with and for the pastor each day during my visit to his church. When I ask him if I might pray with him prior to the morning worship, he is sometimes taken aback by the suggestion. None have ever refused, however, and all are very appreciative. Is this meaningful or effective? All I know is that when all is said and done, word drifts back to me that of all the things I did during my visit, one of the most significant was to spend time in prayer with the pastor.

Based on that feedback, I believe that one effective means of pastoring a pastor would be for the elders of the church to gather with the pastor for five or ten minutes prior to the morning worship to pray that God will empower him and fill him with the Holy Spirit as he ministers to the congregation. It is also important to pray for the choir and the congregation as they make their way into the sanctuary. Prayer for the Sunday school, children, teachers, and the program is important as well. The time prior to worship is powerful. It's a time that will slow the rushing mind of the pastor and help him to focus on what is before him. It is a time when the leaders of the church are bound together heart-to-heart in prayer, and it is a time when the pastor can be pastored.

This is something that can't be legislated or mandated; it has to be an act of the heart. Church leaders who feel led need to find their way to the pastor's study, lay hands on him, and pray.

Praying for the pastor does not need to be limited to just Sunday morning. If the pastor is experiencing difficult times, members of the congregation praying for him will comfort and pastor him more than people will ever know.

The pastor's role is a very public one, and though all of the congregation may feel close to him, the feeling is not the same for him. *He cannot and will not feel close to every person in his congregation.* Those that are a part of his inner circle are the ones that stand the best chance of being received as a pastor. The rest of the congregation must be content to pastor from a distance.

> *But what to those who find? Ah, this,*
> *No tongue or pen can show;*
> *The love of Jesus, what it is,*
> *None but His loved ones know.*

CHAPTER 5

REV., DR., D.D., D.MIN., PH.D., TH.D., ETC.

"He has shown you, O man, what is good; And what does the Lord require of you but to act justly, To love mercy, And to walk humbly with your God?"
                                        —*Micah 6:8*

Sorting through my mail one afternoon, a small envelope caught my eye. I could tell it was a personal note from a pastor. Across the top of the notepaper was the pastor's name followed by "Th.M., D.D., S.T.D., L.L.D." As if that were not enough, under his name was written "Senior Minister." That told me far more about the person than the two sentences comprising the text of the note.

It is not the number of titles after a pastor's name

that makes him effective as he pastors a large church. The titles might give entry to certain churches or positions, but they certainly won't hold him there.

Degrees or titles may be very impressive to some people and very intimidating to others. They have a ring of prestige, power, and success. The pastor mentioned is prominent and well known. When his name is mentioned, people automatically think of him as prestigious, powerful, and successful. I suppose he is successful, if the success of ministry is measured by the numbers of people added to a congregation, the size of the church budget, the number of people on staff, and the number of new buildings that have been built. *Degrees may shape the mind and intellect of the pastor, but Christ molds the heart and soul.* It is from the heart and soul that vision and ministry flow.

The pastor fills many different roles in the church. He is not only the shepherd of the flock, he is also the chief executive officer of a large organization, overseer of the budget, president of the board. He is faced with making the same kind of decisions that executives are faced with in the marketplace.

As a pastor enters ministry, he often pastors in a small church or as a solo pastor. In these situations he fills many roles. It is not unusual for pastors to type the bulletin, sweep out the sanctuary, lead the singing, preach the sermon, and turn off the lights at the end of the morning. In larger churches, some of these roles are filled by staff members, and the senior pastor assumes a variety of different roles again.

PASTOR OR ADMINISTRATOR

When a pastor moves to a church that requires a multiple staff ministry, he is called upon perhaps more than ever to use the administrative ability that God has given him. He must administer a staff, a budget, and a program—all of which require a lot of skill and energy. Many pastors who are excellent preachers often lack administrative ability. Some pastors who have excellent administrative skills lack pastoral ability. It is interesting to note that when a pastor who has strong pastoral gifts and poor administrative skills leaves a church, invariably the search committee begins to look for someone who is a good administrator. They will often call a pastor because he has good administrative ability. Soon after that new person assumes the position the congregation says, "We just want to be loved. Can't our pastor love us like the last one did?" They don't understand why this man isn't a lover like his predecessor. And yet during all the years of the former pastor, the congregation griped because he couldn't administer. The new pastor often finds himself on his way out within a short period of time unless he is able to change his style enough to please the congregation. When that congregation searches for that pastor's replacement, they will call someone who will love them, and the cycle goes on.

Pastors often struggle with managing their time. Part of the problem comes from interruptions by their flock. The congregation views these not as interruptions but as part of his job. He is there to minister to and care for the flock. When a person is in crisis and needs the pastor's counsel, care, and prayers, that is his first priority. But often well-meaning people drop by simply to visit with him, without considering the work on his desk awaiting his attention.

It is traditionally thought in pastoral circles that to do adequate preaching requires one hour of preparation for every minute that is preached. When members of the congregation wonder what the pastor does all week, they forget the amount of time and energy that goes into preparing a meaningful worship experience. In addition to Sunday worship, if he is teaching a Bible study or a midweek class or is leading a retreat he needs preparation time for them as well. Handling correspondence, working with staff, managing a budget, and dealing with day-to-day problems ensure a full week for pastors.

How important are the degrees and titles to Jane and Joe Pewsitter? The string of degrees may impress a search committee, but once the pastor is installed and launches ministry, the degrees are no longer a factor. Jane and Joe Pewsitter expect a pastor who can relate to where they are in their walk with Christ. They seek someone who is real, who struggles with some of the same issues they struggle with, who can challenge their spiritual growth, and who can be a model of what the Christian faith is all about. Being able to show the relevancy of the gospel to his congregation is more important than being able to quote theologians of the past. The pastors who communicate a real, living, pulsating faith experience to their congregation are the ones who are involved in growing churches.

What are the characteristics that we look for in the pastor of a church? A truly effective leader is
- one who has the heart of a servant.
- one who can set a pace for others.
- one who has a sensitive spirit.
- one who can give direction.
- one who leads by example.
- one who will not ask someone to do something he wouldn't do himself.

- one who is assertive, but not aggressive.
- one who dares to dream.
- one who can plan ahead.
- one who will see a project through to its completion.
- one who can successfully motivate others.
- one who knows how to laugh and cry.
- one who can bring out the best in people.
- one who can be confident in others.
- one who dares to trust God in all that he does.

"Just as the Son of Man did not come to be served, but to serve, and to give His life a ransom for many" (Matt. 20:28).

Jane, a committed Christian, had been actively involved in her church for over thirty years. Through the years she had experienced mountaintop experiences in the faith as well as plateaus and valleys. But there came a time in her life when she simply did not have the answers to questions in her life and her past. She began to discuss these things with her pastor, and over a period of time he helped her to see some things in her life that needed to be dealt with and healed by God. Her pastor quietly walked with her through valleys of pain and struggle and into the light of wholeness and strength. He not only taught her about the never-ending love of Christ but also helped her to experience true forgiveness and freedom that only Christ can provide. He taught her, he prayed with her, he listened to her, he held her accountable, and he kept her eyes focused on the living Christ.

Jane knew that she had not been baptized as an infant or as a believer. After all that she had experienced in drawing closer to Christ, it became important to her to be baptized, to be publicly claimed by Him.

And so it was one warm August afternoon, just before dusk, that Jane and her husband and the pastor and his family stood on the shore of Long Island Sound, read the Scripture, and prayed together. Leaving family and friends behind, the pastor and Jane waded out into the waters of the sound. In taking those steps, Jane left every earthly thing behind and walked into the arms of Jesus Christ. She heard her pastor saying, "I baptize you in the name of the Father and of the Son and of the Holy Spirit," and as she went under the water she knew that she had been cleansed, claimed, forgiven, and loved as a child of God.

At that moment all of the academic degrees in the world meant nothing to Jane. All that mattered was that a minister of the gospel of Jesus Christ cared enough to come alongside her and minister to her at her point of need. That pastor, for Jane, exemplifies Micah 6:8, "And what does the Lord require of you but to act justly, To love mercy, And to walk humbly with your God?"

Success in ministry is measured in changed lives, not in numbers of people and budget dollars and fancy buildings. All those things may come and go, but lives changed for Christ are forever. Jane's pastor is a quiet, humble man who serves God faithfully in a small to midsize congregation. Few people will know the impact his ministry had on Jane's life. He dares to be and do what God calls him to be and do. Prestige, power, and success mean nothing if the personalness, the heart of ministry, and the touch of the people are sacrificed. For Jane, she saw in her pastor what Leslie Weatherhead said so well:

> For me 'twas not the truth you taught
> To you so clear, to me so dim,

But when you came to me you brought
A sense of Him.
And from your eyes He beckons me,
And from your heart His love is shed,
Till I lose sight of you—and see
The Christ instead. *

---

*Leslie Weatherhead, *Jesus and Ourselves* (New York: Abingdon-Cokesbury Press, n.d.), p. 232.

CHAPTER 6

PASTOR SPELLED L-A-D-Y!

"You did not choose Me, but I chose you and appointed you that you should go and bear fruit, and that your fruit should remain."

—John 15:16

My husband and I stepped into the narthex of a little Presbyterian church in Ventura, California. As he signed the guestbook, I caught the eye of my dear friend Esther as she walked across the sanctuary to greet us. With a marvelous smile and a twinkle in her eye, she said, "Can you believe this is happening to me? I am about to be ordained for the pastoral ministry. God really does have a sense of humor!"

Esther and I have been friends for over twenty years. She is a preacher's kid, an energetic and enthusiastic Christian woman. When our children were babies, we shared a car pool to the church for women's meetings. She began a neighborhood Bible study, and as the children approached school age, she decided to pick up some courses at Fuller Seminary to assist her in teaching a Bible study. The more she studied, the more she wanted to study, until she reached a place where she believed God was calling her into pastoral ministry. Graduation came, and she was called to be an associate pastor in the lovely community of Ventura.

And so the Reverend Mom, in her early forties, began a career that God had been shaping over a period of many years. Now Esther is wife and mother, managing a family of four children, maintaining a large home, and helping a husband who had supported her through the seminary process. She is also pastor of a congregation, and like so many women today, Esther is juggling two careers.

She has a pastor's heart and genuinely cares for people in her flock. Though more mature, she remains the same fun-loving, enthusiastic, energetic woman she always has been.

Esther is an excellent model of what women in the ordained ministry are like. The most effective women that I have known in ordained ministry have been women who are secure in their identity and who lead a well-balanced life. Many are happily married with families and have responded to the call of God. Not many have sought the pastorate; most have been led to it. These women bring compassion and strength to ministry. They are hardworking and usually know how to get things done. They are skilled at putting people together, getting committees to function, and setting people free to do ministry. Many of them bring a good listening ear that facilitates a caring or counseling ministry. Members of a congregation find them easy to trust and will seek their counsel.

Women bring to the pastoral ministry a wonderful touch that many men don't have. They bring caring and nurturing gifts that reach to the heartstrings of a congregation. They are excellent counselors who can evaluate a situation quickly and confront the person with the problem. Then they go the extra mile and walk with them until the problem is resolved. They bring strength, empathy, and compassion in ways that few men can.

Generally, women are extremely hardworking and conscientious, willing to take on a role and give it great energy. Many are creative and innovative, not being content with a successful program, but always looking for ways to improve it. They are usually good students of the Word and more disciplined toward study and personal growth than many men. For the most part, they are well organized in their work and are adept administrators. They know how to involve people.

Not all the women who seek calls into the pastoral ministry have these admirable characteristics. I have seen some women move into ordination for all of the wrong reasons. Disenchanted with a career in the marketplace, some women have entered seminary with the idea that the pastorate will be better than what they experienced in the business world. Some have had extremely unhappy experiences in their personal lives and have looked to careers in the church to solve their problems. What they fail to realize is that they carry their problems with them into ministry.

These are the women who bring anger, frustration, pain, and failure with them into seminary and develop the attitude that "by God I have earned the right to be pastor, therefore, I will be." Hearing the still small voice of God calling them into ministry is not a factor in these women's decisions.

It is important to note that some men enter seminary for the same reasons and have just as many personality flaws as women. But because the ministry has been a male-dominated career for so long, men's flaws are often overlooked, while the women's flaws are highly magnified.

Women often are called to serve tiny rural churches, yoked churches, campus ministry chaplaincies, and multistaff churches as associates. That is also where most men begin. At present, only a small number of women have become senior pastors or heads of staff in large churches. This is largely due to the fact that women have not been in ordained ministry long enough to work their way up to that level.

When it comes to serving as a solo pastor in a tiny rural church or in a campus ministry, the pastor has only the constituency to deal with. In many instances, she can shape ministry almost any way she wants and often gets excellent response from her congregation.

In a large church, when a woman becomes an associate, she faces many of the same dynamics that she would have faced in the marketplace. She is subordinate to a head of staff, usually a male. She is expected to work and minister within certain expectations. She is to be accountable for her work. For women who struggled with these dynamics in another career, ministry can be difficult. But now she is confronted with these painful truths in the church that was to be her "safe" place where she could succeed.

Some women who are gifted educators and counselors have moved into the ordained ministry because the ordination provides for them a better standard of living. Tax-free housing and other benefits are available for those who are ordained but are not available for other professionals in ministry.

Years ago, many women studied to be directors of Christian education and became the backbone of religious education in our country. Today, those same women are studying for the ordained ministry because the salary and benefits are better and because the position carries more status. Some women become pastors of education, but many opt to move into other areas of ministry, leaving openings and opportunities in the role of Christian educator.

Some ordained women have moved a step beyond the local congregation, and are ministering with great success. Ordained women are found in the legislative and judicial areas of some denominations. Again, they provide leadership and administrative capability and also serve as pastors to other pastors. Women are also highly accepted, acclaimed, and appreciated as seminary professors as well.

Women, whether ordained or lay, are effective in ministry today. It does not require ordination to minister to, to care for, to counsel, to teach, to equip, to disciple, and to nurture others in the Christian faith. These are the very things women have done without recognition through the ages.

Dr. Henrietta C. Mears was a high-school chemistry teacher when she was called as director of Christian education at the First Presbyterian Church of Hollywood, California. She arrived at the church as a young woman and spent her life developing the Christian education program in that church. Her concept of

Christian education laid the foundation for the Sunday school as we know it in America today. She began to write curriculum when she could not find adequate material, and Gospel Light Press was born. She trained teachers to teach. She provided resources and rooms for the growing classes. But perhaps more importantly, she developed young people for ministry. She was an amazing woman!

Her favorite class was the college class, and though she was responsible for the education of eight thousand church members, she kept hands-on responsibility for the collegians. They loved her and fondly called her "Teacher." She was a gracious woman, immaculately dressed and coiffed. Gentle and kind, she took a sincere interest in people as she pastored them, taught them, and counseled them.

She was quiet in manner, until she stood up to teach. Standing no more than five feet one inch or so, she would proclaim the gospel with great vigor and strength. She challenged people with the truth of the gospel. She let them know the Christian life was not an easy life to live. At one point in her ministry, it was estimated that more than four hundred fifty men and women had gone into some area of ministry as a result of her witness to them. There was a time when she could travel anywhere in the world, and one of her former students would meet her at the airport. As a result of her ministry, thousands of people came to Christ, and though she went to glory more than twenty-five years ago, there are people going into full-time ministry today because they have been touched by someone in whom she invested time many years ago.

Over and over she would challenge her students to find their place marked *X*. She taught that God would lead them and give them the desires in their hearts to be where He wanted them to be. When speaking at conferences, rallies, or classes, she would often close her message by challenging her audience to pray the prayer, "Lord, what wilt thou have me to do? Not my church, not my minister, not my friends—but me! Lord what wilt thou have me to do—today?"

Miss Mears was a *lady* in the true sense of the word. I have never met another person quite like her. She was unique. She never sought ordination, but she pastored multitudes. She never sought power or success, but dozens of Christian organizations have been established as a result of her ministry. Toward the end of her life, someone asked her what she would do differently if she had it to do all over again. She thought a moment and said, "I would trust God completely." She was an excellent model of what men and women in ministry, ordained or lay, can be like if their eyes are focused on Christ.

Women like Henrietta Mears, now a legend, and my friend Esther have made a difference in ministry today. There is a need and a place for women to take an active role in ministry, ordained or not. The prayer I pray for all those going into ministry, male or female, lay or ordained, is the prayer Paul prayed in the third chapter of Ephesians. I pray "that He would grant you, according to the riches of His glory, to be strengthened with might through His Spirit in the inner man, that Christ may dwell in your hearts through faith; that you, being rooted and grounded in love, may be able to comprehend with all the saints what is the width and length and depth and height—to know the love of Christ which passes knowledge; that you may be filled with all the fullness of God" (vv. 16–19).

CHAPTER 7

POTSHOTS FROM THE PEW

"A bruised reed He will not break."
—*Isaiah 42:3*

The call came early one summer morning. "Dave needs you to come. Two associates and the director of music have resigned. He wants you to help him think through staffing for the next five years. How soon can you get here?"

Two weeks passed before I could clear my schedule and spend time with my friend. By the time I arrived, he was experiencing mixed emotions about his situation. He was neither heartbroken nor surprised that the three had resigned—in fact, he was expecting it. Each had served more than five years; they had met the challenge and it was time to take another call. Dave had been aware that they were in the search process and had supported them as they took the next steps in their career. But he did not expect that all three would resign within days of each other.

The church had experienced great growth during the previous eight years. It was the second fastest growing church in a mainline denomination. For that to happen dedication and hard work are required on the part of the staff. The two associates and the music director had done a noble job, but they had done all they could do. They had taken their ministries as far as they could and had reached the point where they were doing maintenance ministry. They exemplified the principle that it is impossible to lead someone farther than where you have been.

Dave was a visionary who had unlimited hopes and plans for the church, but his staff could not put flesh on those dreams.

Some time had passed since the resignations had been announced, and now the first wave of "potshots from the pew" were launched directly at the senior pastor.

Potshots come in various sizes, shapes, and forms. The first one was a subtle but direct two-page letter from an elder just wanting to let the pastor know that as a result of "his forcing those people out," *many* people had left the church and *some* were showing their unhappiness by cutting back their giving. He also implied that the pastor had indeed "pulled the plug" on those people. The writer also implied he was merely fulfilling his duty to inform the pastor; that the pastor more than likely still had his support, while all other support was falling away from him.

The *tongue-in-cheek* potshot showed up in the choir newsletter. A rather crude article, written in satire by our friend "Anonymous," concluded that the director had been run off. This was an extremely divisive potshot at a time when much healing was needed in the choir.

The *party-line* potshot was probably one of the most devastating of all. Two friends phoned each other with a story, embellished it a bit, shared it with another, and so forth. Each time the story was told, it got juicier and farther from the truth.

The *inquiring-minds-want-to-know* potshot came from a church member who called to let the pastor know he was doing his best to defend him, but didn't quite understand how the pastor could allow this to happen.

The *Christian-corrective* potshot appeared in letter form several days after the first letter. This one was brief and to the point. Written in Christian language it sharply criticized the pastor and used Scripture to somehow justify the attack.

Though these comments were isolated and relatively few, they wounded the pastor. None of the people who had taken potshots had bothered to take the time to ask the pastor what happened. No one stopped to think that he, too, might have been taken by surprise. No one gave any thought to the fact that the pastor might have been hurt or upset. They merely launched the potshots.

As I listened to Dave share these instances, it reminded me again of the lonely position senior pastors hold and how they are so often misunderstood. It is so simple to jump to conclusions and say or write things we soon regret. Nevertheless, those comments are sharper than a two-edged sword.

This is a classic scenario that gets played out consistently in large churches. The names, the titles, and the potshots may change, but the result is still the same. The senior pastor comes out looking like the bad guy. What do pastors do when the potshots fly? Few shrug them off and go on as usual. Some might like to think they do that very thing, but they soon realize they can't lay the negative words aside.

Most get angry, and that anger manifests itself in many ways. Some yell, some weep, some go for a long drive, some jog or walk. Some sit down and talk to a trusted friend. Some take it all inward, don't process it, go on as usual, and suffer health consequences later.

At a time like this, probably all of them ponder whether it is time to seek another call. Suddenly the little two-hundred-member church looks very appealing, and they think they would be problem-free there. They think they could preach and teach to their heart's content and not be plagued by these things.

Congregations fail to realize that pastors have sensitive feelings and that in their capacity as pastors they tend to be more open and, therefore, more vulnerable to criticism than most. *Somehow the people in the pew seem to think they can say anything they like to the pastor and it won't change how he views them or ministers to them.*

It is astounding how often well-meaning parishioners—in the name of Christ—will strip down a pastor, expect him to take it, and, of course, change his ways instantly to fit their demands. This kind of treatment usually is initiated by people who know just enough about the situation to be dangerous and don't care to know the whole story for fear it might save the attack on the pastor. *They tend to resemble vultures feasting on a fresh kill.*

In Dave's case, he was shocked, discouraged, angry, and depressed. As he shared the sequence of events and the various potshots, the hurt became more and more apparent and he finally said, "Maybe it's time for me to leave."

As we talked, he knew he couldn't just leave. It is not that simple in his denomination. What he needed more than anything at that moment was a vote of affirmation from the leadership of the church.

As I began to talk with him about configuring a staff for the next five years, he slowly dragged his heart out of the pit and began to think creatively. But every time his mind wandered, he slowly fell back into his frustrated state.

We were to meet with the combined planning and staff personnel committees that evening, and I wondered what he would communicate to them. Would he share some of his pain and allow the leadership to minister to him? Or would he press on as if nothing had happened to lay out his dream for the future. I couldn't guess which way he would go.

The conference room was full of the prime leaders in the church. Seated around that table were some of the most influential people in the church and in the community. They were committed Christians accustomed to the rough-and-tumble corporate world who get potshots directed at them on a regular basis.

The pastor opened the meeting with prayer and then proceeded to share with the group some of the events of the past weeks. They had known that the movement of staff was coming. But as the pastor unfolded the backlash, the band of men and women slowly began to respond. First, they moaned as the pastor shared his story; then they exchanged glances and shook their heads. The pastor concluded his brief remarks, with the comment that perhaps he ought to move on as well.

Slowly and steadily, each one expressed surprise that anyone felt this way and then affirmed the pastor in his ministry. When everyone had addressed this issue, they instructed the pastor to "stuff" the negatives and get on with showing them his ideas for the future. The pastor moved to his flip chart and began to show the leaders what he was envisioning. They heard his plan, raised a few questions for clarification, and said, "Let's get on with it."

Those few moments of affirmation and forward thinking were enough to get him started in a positive direction one more time.

Why do things like this happen? Often, without thinking, we allow hurtful comments to fly. Sometimes when we are in a crisis ourselves we tend to lash out at those who would be our best source of help.

When the pastor or staff members are under a heavy strain, that is the time to come alongside them and offer them support and encouragement. Having an accurate account of the whole story is important before beginning to offer constructive comment. If criticism must be brought, it must be spoken in truth and love; confrontation must be honest, tender, and compassionate.

Negative comments are destructive and diminish much that would be good. The classic comment to the pastor as he greets people at the close of worship, "It was a good sermon, pastor, but a little long," is not humorous. You can be sure the pastor heard only "but a little long" and carried that around for a few days. I have long since ceased to be amazed at some of the criticisms parishioners share with me about their pastor or members of staff. People have complained to me that the pastor's Bible is worn out and they wish he would buy a new one. Others complain about the clothes he wears, or that he needs a haircut, or that he doesn't turn his microphone off when he sings and he can't carry a tune.

As the people in the pew, if we would provide affirmation and encouragement on a regular basis, our pastors and leaders would be far more effective than when they must constantly deal with negative-thinking parishioners.

The congregation never knew Dave's frustration about his staff. They never knew that the church was slipping into maintenance ministry. They never knew that immediately prior to the resignations Dave had given serious thought to taking a call to another church. He had been approached by several fine churches, but he did not get a clear leading from the Lord to pursue a change. He and his wife made it a serious matter of prayer. Though they had prayed about the possibility of leaving, they had not prayed about whether they should stay. Finally, they asked the Lord what they should do. They were willing to leave if that was what the Lord wanted. They were willing to stay if that was what the Lord wanted. All they asked was that He show them His will. The three resignations came two days later as the Lord's way of saying, "Stay and build ministry bigger and stronger to my glory."

On the way to the airport, I asked Dave how his sermon was coming for Sunday. "Good," he said with gusto. "It's called 'Starting Over!'"

"I will give you a new heart and put a new spirit within you" (Ezek. 36:26).

CHAPTER 8

PEW PARALYSIS, OR SHACKLED BY SHORT-SIGHTED SINNERS!

"It is not the size of the steeple, but the size of the heart of the people that determines success."

"He who opens and no one shuts, and shuts and no one opens: I know your works. See, I have set before you an open door, and no one can shut it."

—Revelation 3:7–8

One of the most discouraging moments in ministry occurs when a visionary pastor shares his dreams and goals and members of his congregation respond with a we'll-watch-you-do-it attitude.

A small congregation tends to fall into a routine or a comfortable pattern of doing things. Over a period of years, they begin to think that is the way they've always done it, and that is the way it will always be done. Pastors and members may come and go, but the thinking generally remains the same. It is a comfort zone for many folks, and it is difficult for them to face and accept change.

SMALL CHURCH MENTALITY

The church may grow to a midsize congregation and eventually to a large church. Unless major changes have occurred, however, the small church mentality will continue to be a stumbling block to a church becoming all that God intends.

Small-church mentality is often found in people who have joined the church a number of years earlier. Instead of growing in their concept and view of the church over the years, their view is the same as when they entered the church ten, fifteen, or twenty years ago. They are rather shortsighted and tend to remember how it was in the "good old" days. They firmly resist change. They want everything to be just as it was when they came into the membership of the church. Because our culture and environment are constantly changing, the church also must change to meet the needs of the people.

People with small-church mentality in positions of leadership in the church can steal a pastor's dream and discourage him to the point of his taking a call to another church that is ready to move forward with him. Pastors get tired of doing battle with the days gone by. If people are not open to stretch their vision and look forward to the things of the future, ministry becomes extremely difficult.

During a question-and-answer time at a leadership retreat, one elder asked how to increase the attendance at the 8:30 A.M. worship service. This church had two morning worship services with Sunday school between the two services. The long-standing tradition had been one worship service at 11:00 A.M., but when the sanctuary could no longer hold everyone, they added the second service. Though reasonably well attended, there was concern among the leadership about how to strengthen it. It was a duplicate service, except they did not seat a choir for the first service. A full music ministry serves to complete a good worship experience. Though a soloist may be excellent, it is not the same to ears who have listened to a choral anthem for years. When I pointed this out, the leadership could quickly see that and heartily responded, "Yes, we will tell the music director to whip up another choir."

While they were resting on that thought, I asked how many of the present leaders attended the first service. None. That spoke volumes about how they felt about the additional service. I told them that if at least half of them would attend the first service, it would add leadership strength and support and provide more empty seats for visitors at the late service.

They argued, "But we have always worshiped at 11:00 A.M., and we wouldn't get to see our friends if we went to early worship." They remembered when they knew everyone in church, and now the church had grown to a size where everyone couldn't possibly know everyone. The small-church mentality was preventing this church from growing. Unless this mentality is overcome, the church will continue to do maintenance ministry and will not grow.

Pastors will gain the verbal support of their congregation and move forward with a project, but the true vote comes when it is time to put the money, time, and energy into it. People vote with their pocketbooks and their energy. And although they may say yes with their lips, they may say no with their wallets and their involvement. I believe that as Christians we owe it to the Lord, to ourselves, and to the pastor of the church to be honest and that we vote the way we speak and feel. If we do say yes, we ought to put our money where our mouths are. If we are in favor of the new project or ministry and simply cannot support it financially, we should at least affirm the pastor and the leadership for the direction in which they are moving. Verbal support helps make the work easier.

Folks who vote negatively for a project will often reflect their votes in their attitudes. They pull back their moral support. Once active in midweek activities, they now attend less frequently. Once regular ushers, they now are not available. Once committed Sunday school teachers, they now are substitutes or do not teach at all. Once active in the choir, they now give others the opportunity. Once hearty handshakers, they now exit by other doors. They let friends know they are not happy with the direction of the church. Usually, in all of this, they find people who support their thinking, and the rumble and fallout gets a little louder. In time, the pastor hears that there is a rumble in the congregation, but he doesn't understand where it has originated or why. By the time it gets back to him, a thunder storm has been formed out of a rumble. If the disgruntled members had talked directly with the pastor about their feelings, much frustration could have been avoided.

My day had been full of appointments with members of the congregation. I had heard just about every tale of woe possible from people generally unhappy with their church. They were unhappy with everything from the pastor to the color of the carpet. But the final straw came when a couple in their sixties came to speak with me. He was a retired businessman, and they had been active members in the church for many years. He had served as treasurer and was very concerned about the financial situation of the church. We talked about it at great length, and he sounded his case for planning a realistic budget. He simply could not understand how people could pledge to the budget and not support it. Finally, he and his wife indicated that they had just become so frustrated with the entire financial picture that they were simply holding back their pledge until the church could get its act together. They were causing part of the problem that they were so concerned about. They were voting with their wallet.

Members of a congregation need to ask themselves, "Are we a load that our pastor must drag, or are we a lift to his ministry?"

A pastor spends great amounts of time and energy trying to communicate to a congregation a vision and direction for the future. When a pastor tells a congregation that the church needs a new roof, the carpet needs repairing, or a new sanctuary must be built, all too often the congregation views him as another "kingdom builder" because, from their perspective, everything is all right. But when the roof leaks during the first rain or someone has a terrible fall because of the worn carpet, then people wonder why this hasn't been taken care of.

One pastor told me that he talked to his congregation for several years about enlarging the sanctuary. They had moved to several worship services and had outgrown the space in the aged structure. When the roof caved in during a winter storm, the congregation finally took the pastor seriously and took steps to build a new sanctuary. Even then it was an uphill battle to get a building designed and built to meet the many desires of the church family. One person wrote a check to cover the cost of the carpeting throughout the new structure—a very generous gift indeed. However, he insisted on selecting the color of the carpet. Unfortunately, what he wanted and what the interior designer recommended were at opposite ends of the spectrum. The selection committee sided with the interior designer's choice, and the man tore up the check. I wonder what the true motive was behind the man's generous offer. Was it to see a need and meet it? Or was it to be in control and call attention to himself?

Pastors regularly face members of their congregation who want to be in control. A few members can form a power structure that can be a positive force or a negative force.

THE SPIRIT OF DIVISIVENESS

There is a divisive spirit within some congregations. Honest, caring Christians come to me and express utter frustration when they encounter this divisiveness. Divisiveness feeds on the negative. If something is less than perfect, divisiveness will turn it into a major negative issue.

If something new is developed in ministry, a divisive nature will find enough fault to make it fail. If ministry is provided to groups outside the church as a means of outreach, a divisive spirit will point out the high cost of wear and tear on facilities and will work to shut out these groups. If a qualified staff is hired to build ministry, a divisive spirit will throw stumbling blocks in the way so that ministry never becomes all that it could.

Divisiveness is probably the most destructive force found in a church today. The source is usually found in a small core of people. Those people, often without realizing it, work harder at destroying something than at building it up. Because of their enthusiasm for the church and their zeal to make everything "right" in their eyes, they are usually involved in almost every area of the church. It is difficult for the members of the church family to be involved without being tainted by the divisive thrust.

Divisiveness spreads through gossip. Truth is embellished with innuendoes, hearsay, and personal conclusions that make the story very convincing. *Divisiveness, in its most effective form, cloaks its actions in the Scripture.* Scripture is manipulated to fit each instance and is preached to receptive people until they cave in.

Divisiveness is so subtle that people do not know they are being sucked into it. Divisiveness is intimidating and controlling. As it becomes stronger, the congregation grows more apathetic and complacent.

Divisiveness is the driving force that splits a church. A divisive spirit can be diminished and eventually eliminated if faced head-on. *The elders or those in leadership positions have the responsibility and authority to rebuke those who would tear down what God is raising up.* They must be strong and of good courage. When they hear gossip, they must shut it down. Strength will weaken and reduce a divisive spirit. If there is division among the elders or leaders, it must be dealt with before it reduces the leadership to frustration, apathy, and resignation.

PUT UP OR SHUT UP

The pastor had led his congregation for almost twenty years and had weathered every kind of crisis imaginable in the church. He had walked with his people through good times and bad. His preaching remained fresh each week, and he continued to put forth the vision of ministry to his congregation. He had heard every gripe in the book more times than he could remember.

It was then Stewardship Sunday. Over the past thirty years, I have heard my share of stewardship sermons, but I will not forget the message I heard from this pastor. He had preached eloquently the message of being good stewards of all that God has given us. It was powerful and challenged the congregation to be cheerful tithers. He closed his sermon with prayer, stepped down out of the pulpit, and moved to a position directly in front of the congregation. It was there that he said what he had been feeling for many years.

He looked directly at his congregation and said that he was tired of hearing people complain about the program of the church, about the staff, about the facilities, about any new ministry that was launched. That kind of language was holding the church back. He went on to say that the loudest voices of complaint were those who did not show any record of giving to the church. Then he said what most pastors would like to say and won't: "May I suggest that if you cannot financially support this church, you go to a church that you will support." With that the congregation cheered.

People will withdraw from the church for more reasons than disagreement with issues. Personal crises will often draw people closer to the church, but for others it drives them farther from it. People will pull back from their involvement in church when a marriage is in trouble, a career is in crisis, or there are problems with children. They are afraid to let others know their pain. They fear they will be thought of as unacceptable or not good Christians.

It is during times such as these that a pastor and congregation need to reach out with love, to bring care, counsel, and support during a time of crisis.

Occasionally we see a congregation that wants to move forward with vigor but the pastor tends to hold them back. In situations such as this, usually the pastor is more a plodder and less a visionary. He may be comfortable leading the church as it is but is fearful to risk what is needed to move it to new heights. This happens in churches where the pastor has been there a number of years and may be near retirement. He may be somewhat weary from ministry and may just want to spend the remaining years of ministry comfortably. If the congregation is progressive and enthusiastic, they may not be willing to accept this style of leadership. The pastor's last years will be miserable instead of comfortable as he had planned.

The ideal situation is for a pastor to be a visionary, pacesetter, and leader. He should be far enough in front of the congregation that they will follow, but not so far that they lose sight of him. Every pastor hopes to lead a congregation that is responsive to the vision and shares ownership in it, is receptive to the gospel and reproduces their faith in others, and is open to grow and change in order to meet the needs of the community around them.

Ray Ortlund wrote in *Let the Church Be the Church,*

> What ought to be the goals of a local church? What should the staff and leaders decide on as their church's biblical objectives? How do they get their people committed to the right things? How do they get their local fellowship prioritized?
> Unless we ask this question we'll aim at nothing—and hit it every time! Often a pastor thinks he's served a church five years or ten years, when actually he's served only one year and repeated his one-year pastorate five times over or ten times over. He has little sense of direction, of going anywhere, and he doesn't lead his people strongly.
> It is important that churches, pastors, staffs, and church leaders develop a philosophy of ministry, a direction, a definition of who they are and where they're going together. What is needed today are congregations that understand their unique purpose as a church and concentrate on fulfilling that function.

For this to happen, everyone must lay aside their own personal agendas and trust that God will mold and shape the future of the church. It is in sacrificing ourselves that we are saved. It is in giving that we receive. It is in loving that we are loved.

"If you will take care of the things that are dear to God. He will take care of the things that are dear to you" (Alice Taylor).

CHAPTER 9

STAFFING TO SUCCEED OR FAIL!

"If you can talk with crowds and keep your
   virtue,
or walk with Kings—nor lose the common
   touch;
If neither foes nor loving friends can hurt
   you;
If all men count with you, but none too
   much . . ."

—Rudyard Kipling

AN ALTER EGO

This was the third day of interviewing the members of staff at First Church. The pastor's administrative assistant sat across the conference table from me.

As I listened to her share her concerns about the staff and its structure, she asked me why a certain person was a member of the staff. "I really don't understand why he is here. What does he do?" This was an interesting question for a longtime staff member to ask of a newcomer. I thought for a moment and then responded, "Don't you see that he is your boss's alter ego?" Her lovely face broke into a smile and she said, "Of course, I see that now that you have mentioned it, but I certainly would never have thought of it."

Senior pastors of large churches can not be everything to everyone. The scope of ministry is too vast for them to be and to do all of what they would do in a smaller setting. *Though I am convinced they never consciously search for and hire a person who is their alter ego, many successful pastors in large churches have a staff member who fills that description.* That person may be an associate pastor, a lay professional, the pastor's secretary, or an administrative assistant. When there is someone like that in place, the pastor's ministry tends to run more smoothly and the congregation feels more fulfilled by the ministry he offers them.

The senior pastor of a large church is a man with a complex career. He must spend great portions of time in preparation for preaching and in setting direction for his congregation. But he is also the chief executive officer of a fast-moving business. He must direct his staff and meet with committees and leaders. As pastor of a large church, he often has responsibilities in the community, in a seminary, or at a higher denominational level. He is called upon to speak at conferences and assist smaller struggling churches. In filling those responsibilities, some of the gentle shepherd characteristics become secondary and preaching, administrative, and leadership gifts become primary. He becomes less available to his parishioners. He might even be viewed as a tough taskmaster by his staff.

The person who is the pastor's alter ego is an extension of his personality, stepping to the same drumbeat and sharing a common heart and vision for ministry. It is not the position description that defines the pastor's alter ego but the personality, heart, and style. If the senior pastor lacks gentleness, perceptivity, and understanding, this person provides it. If the senior pastor lacks administrative or organizational strength, the alter ego has that gift and enhances the pastor's ministry. It is this staff person who completes the pastor in who he is and what his ministry is all about.

If the senior pastor is secure in who he is, he can usually recognize his weak spots. He would be wise to staff to meet those weaknesses and not his strengths. For instance, if he is not particularly gifted as a counselor or caregiver, he should hire a staff person to do counseling and provide care to the congregation. Once that person is in place, the pastor can move on to other things.

The same thing applies in the area of administration. If he is not a gifted administrator, then hiring a person to see to the day-to-day administration is to the advantage of the church as well as the pastor. A senior pastor who is insecure in self-worth takes it as a personal failure when he is not an adequate counselor or administrator. At this point, that ego and the competitive spirit enter the picture, and what could have been a good staffing relationship slowly falls apart until both parties are miserable. Though he may delegate responsibility, he may not delegate the authority to get the job done. Therefore, he continues to maintain control.

SECRETARY OR ADMINISTRATIVE ASSISTANT

The hiring of staff often can be delegated to a personnel committee or an administrator. However, the staff position that must be left in the hands of the pastor to hire is his secretary or administrative assistant. That role is an extension of his ministry and personality, and if their hearts don't beat together, the relationship will be difficult at best. Clerical skills are essential, but they are not the measure of an administrative assistant's worth; the people skills make the difference. She must be a good listener, not only to the people contacting the pastor but also to him. She must be self-motivated, perceptive, and decisive. In time, she must know the heart and style of the pastor so well that she can finish the sentences he begins. She must be dependable and trustworthy. She must have a servant's heart.

There will be days that she will listen to him weep and wail about a difficult meeting the night before. She will be called upon to sew a button on his jacket, bring in lunch, search for the right sermon illustration, and give him praise on Monday morning, even if it was only a mediocre sermon the day before. She will know when to interrupt and when to let him wander in the doldrums of running a big church. And at just the right moment, she will take him a hot cup of something or a cold glass of his favorite refresher, spend a few minutes affirming and encouraging him, and he'll be on his way again. She is a true helpmate to the pastor. Although feminists may say these things should not be part of the job description, the caring elements are needed and necessary for some pastors to be most effective.

Yes, I have described the pastor's secretary or administrative assistant's role in feminine language. There are many fine men who fill roles similar to this in industry, but there are few men who fill this role well in the church. The feminine touch brings wisdom and insight and perspective to the pastor that is not generally found in men. The special gift of nurturing is so beautifully found in women, and we see that gift being used in the work of personnel specialists, counselors, therapists, and other care-giving professions.

The person who works outside the pastor's door may be called a secretary, church secretary, pastor's secretary, executive secretary, administrative secretary, or administrative assistant. The qualities and characteristics are the same for each title. The titles vary according to the size of church, size of staff, denomination, and geographical placement in the United States.

When a pastor, associate, or head of staff has someone like this working for him or her, they will be able to develop their ministry to its fullest potential.

THE WE VS. THEY SYNDROME

When the staff of a church is large, an unseen barrier called "the we vs. they syndrome" sometimes appears. One place it is often found is at the doorways to the offices of the senior pastor and his administrative assistant. *The barrier between the inner office and the outer office often can't be seen, but it is certainly always felt.*

The administrative assistant must be loyal to the

senior pastor and is usually closely linked to him. If she is not stable and secure in her relationship to him, she probably will not be able to withstand the barrage of comments, innuendoes, avoidance, and hard looks aimed her way by others.

The assistant's workload is usually very heavy, and pressure is ever present. Seldom will someone volunteer to help her, even though she may come to the aid of others when they are in need. For some reason, other staff members would rather see her sink than to throw her a lifesaver. It is difficult to say why this is so. But after witnessing it consistently in large churches, I am more and more convinced it is a form of jealousy on the part of the staff. They perceive that the administrative assistant has an inside track to the senior pastor, and they wish they had that same relationship. They become determined to reduce the stature they perceive she has, in an effort for all to become equal.

When the pressure is on the administrative assistant, that is often the time she will hear other staff members laughing and talking around the coffee pot. Their workload may not be as intense, but they don't offer to lend a hand. So the administrative assistant works that much harder, coming in early, skipping lunches, and working late. Under the pressure, she withdraws and gets brusque with people. Sometimes she acts like a martyr, which does not help the communication process at all.

Many people are unaware that she is often the secretary for the pastor's family and personal life. Some administrative assistants will be responsible for paying the family bills, banking, making family travel plans, arranging social events, doing family correspondence, and so forth. This may not sound like much, but piling it on an already full desk only adds to the pressure.

The solution is not to give overload work to the support staff. They merely look at it as a castoff from someone who can't keep up with the work, and the rift grows greater. The senior pastor and the administrative assistant should fully evaluate the workload and hire additional help, temporarily or permanently, to relieve the administrative assistant. The administrative assistant can supervise the work being done and delegate additional work.

I also have discovered that when a staff becomes upset with the senior pastor, they tend to take it out on his administrative assistant. If there is tension between the senior pastor and members of staff, they may be very pleasant to each other face to face. But behind the senior pastor's back, the staff directs comments to his administrative assistant.

In the meantime, she also has been on the receiving end of some of her boss's feelings regarding the situation. In many cases the senior pastor has good rapport with his staff, displays a winning personality, and is a lovable kind of guy—but he is not perfect. The imperfections are what drive staff members crazy. Staff members will vent their frustration or anger on the administrative assistant, which gets it off their chests but doesn't harm the relationship everyone feels toward the boss.

Credibility is built when the pastor communicates to the congregation that his administrative assistant will be able to respond to questions or concerns during his absence from the office. She knows his mind. When she speaks she is speaking for the pastor, and people leave her office feeling as though they have talked with him. But he must establish her credibility.

The we vs. they syndrome is found in every area of the church. It usually arises when one area is stressed or overworked and they view another area as "loafing" on the job. "We" becomes more and more important in the mind's eye of those pushed to their limits, and those classed as "they" become more and more the enemy. When this happens, communications break down, and a personnel crisis heats up. If the situation is not dealt with, it soon explodes.

From within the structure, it is difficult to recognize the we vs. they syndrome even when it is at its most heated point. To an outsider with some discernment, it is often quite obvious. The solution is to get communication going again. To do this, it usually requires an objective, thinking person to listen to the frustrations of those involved and to help them understand the other person's perspective. A strong dose of encouragement and affirmation helps quiet things and goes a long way in promoting a willingness on the part of everyone to work together.

If at the core of all of this there is more than an attitude problem, then that issue must be dealt with as well. For example, if the work is not spread evenly, or if a person is not doing a good job, or if the working environment is less than adequate, then those things must be remedied before there can be a permanent solution to the we vs. they syndrome.

DON'T LOOK A GIFT HORSE IN THE MOUTH

Jim, a senior pastor in his late fifties, had invited me to do a study in his church. We spent a great deal of time together during the first few days, and he shared with me the love and tenderness he felt for his two associates. They were very young, and this was their first church to serve after graduating from the seminary. Jim valued these two young men and had great hope in them for the future. He said he had put up with a lot, but he felt it was worth it as he watched them grow and develop strength in ministry.

As I became acquainted with the two associates, I began to realize that their feelings were not mutual toward Jim. In fact, they had a field day demeaning him several times while talking to me. After a while it seemed that no matter what Jim did, in the eyes of the associates it was all wrong. They ridiculed him and mimicked him until I finally suggested that they were perhaps being a little hard on him. But they felt they were right and certainly didn't want any input from me.

Several times a year, those associates would receive anonymous gifts of cash so they could purchase new suits, new shoes, or winter coats. They were always delighted to receive the gifts and even flaunted them a bit in Jim's face since they knew he hadn't received the same envelope. *They never figured out that they flaunted the gift in the face of the giver.*

This illustration is one of dozens that could be written. The gift might be the cost of counseling for a staff person in crisis, the cost of education for an associate's child, or simply the cost of lunch. Whatever it may be, the senior pastor is on the giving end, and the associates or staff are on the receiving end. Soon they begin to expect it, and if a "little treat" doesn't come their way every so often, subtle hints and remarks are made to let the senior pastor know it is time to produce again.

Why does this happen? Perhaps it is paternalism that causes this to develop. Whatever it is, it does not help to build relationships if the same person is always on the giving end.

Staff members need to learn how to give in return. They need to extend the lunch invitation more often than when there is a second agenda brewing. They need to reach out in other ways to those who give to them.

SELECTING STAFF

The most consistent concern raised by senior pastors today focuses on staffing. The issue of staffing—how to hire, who to hire, how to define roles, and how to keep good staff members—consumes more of a senior pastor's time and energy than he would like to give.

During my first evening in Charlie's home, he spent considerable time reviewing his twelve-year ministry at First Church. There were many stories about staff persons that had come and gone, and each tale was filled with frustration, anger, and pain. Finally, I asked him if he had ever known happiness and satisfaction with his staff. Without hesitation he responded, "Never!" He felt as though he had been saddled with inept, incapable, and insubordinate staff throughout his twelve years at that church. His story, unfortunately, is very common.

In Charlie's case, he was partly to blame for his situation, but "the system" was more at fault. The system is that structure within which the particular church functions. A denomination can specify the procedure to follow when calling assistant pastors or hiring other staff members. Even independent churches are sometimes limited by their own constitution. Few churches, if any, leave the hiring of personnel in the hands of the senior pastor. Why? Generally, a congregation does not want him to have too much power.

They say they believe in the committee process; in reality they want to be in control.

Sometimes a search committee will have an ax to grind. Maybe there are one or two people on the committee that are out to get the pastor, either consciously or subconsciously. They search to find an associate pastor to fill a certain job that has been defined. The senior pastor may spend a long time with the person, but that does not always tell a pastor all he needs to know about being able to work together effectively. If he does not give his enthusiastic approval of the candidate, the search committee may override his word and vote to call the associate. This is the committee's way of reprimanding the pastor. In the meantime, the associate goes into a situation where he or she has already been set up to fail. In many instances, a church will pay to move that person across the country and may even provide low-interest loans for housing. The investment and hope in this new staff member is high.

If the new employee doesn't work out and must be asked to leave, the committee will often leave it to the pastor to do the dirty work. In some denominations, it is extremely difficult to remove people from pastoral positions. If the new associate joins the staff, and a period of time goes by before they realize it is not a good situation, it could be several years before that associate moves on. In the meantime, that person has built up a following in the congregation as he was attempting to minister. Through it all, an uncomfortable feeling exists between the senior pastor and the associate. When the associate leaves, some people in the congregation will grieve because he has built some attachments there. Who is made to look like the bad guy in all this? The senior pastor, of course.

The calling and hiring of professional laypeople is similar, but their leave-taking can be far less complicated, if that is the desire of the church.

It is important to keep in mind that no matter who searches, the senior pastor must know the candidate well and feel good about the personality mix and gifts being brought to the position. *If he is careful and thorough in the way he hires, he may not be placed in a position of having to fire.*

The pastor, as head of staff, looks for loyalty, dependability, and trustworthiness in the members of his team. When he has people whom he can not depend on and who are not trustworthy, he finds himself not loyal to them as well.

A pastor and I were discussing how to make staff meetings more effective when he said, "I don't dare open up in front of this bunch because there are three people who would like to devour me. I've reached the point where I don't want to be around them. They are so critical behind my back and pleasant to my face that it is difficult for me to be civil to them." The collegiality of the staff was being sacrificed because three people had a different agenda. He finally told each of them to get on board or leave. All three left within six months, and the senior pastor saw new life come into ministry again.

Pastors of multiple staff churches often find themselves in a trap when members of the staff do not live up to or produce what is expected of them. When staff members are not dependable and trustworthy, a chasm grows between the pastor and a particular member of the staff. Eventually the pastor believes he cannot trust particular people on staff because they have failed to produce ministry when it was expected.

During a staff meeting, if one member is functioning below what is expected, the meeting becomes ineffective. The senior pastor does not communicate as openly, nor is he as trusting to all of the staff, because he knows he has a weak link.

One pastor had two people on his ministry staff that were square pegs in round holes. He could not trust them and wanted them gone. He said he did not feel he could build a team effort while those two remained a part of the staff. It was difficult for him to build cohesiveness, to invite vulnerability, or even to pray with the group because he was so uncomfortable with people he could not trust.

In a situation such as this the pastor often isolates himself. Interestingly enough, most pastors are not aware they are doing this. *When a pastor says, "I don't even feel like I can pray with these people because I can't trust them," that is precisely the time to pray with them, to try to build a better line of communication.* To be joined in prayer requires an openness to one another and to the Lord. It can be difficult for the head of staff to subject himself to in-depth prayer with folks with whom he is so far out of touch, and there's no easy way out of this dilemma. If the break has become too severe, the relationship can't be put back together again. The only way out is for those staff members to move on. By not coming together in prayer, they are severing the spiritual dynamic that could bring forth the healing of a relationship.

PERFORMANCE EVALUATION

A great many churches do not have an adequate process of evaluating performance. In those churches that do have an evaluation procedure, it is often left in the hands of a personnel committee or staff relations committee. Often the senior pastor does not even do an evaluation of his staff. However, if he did, and if he had an evaluation process that was effective, perhaps the seeds of incompatibility would be picked up in this process, rather than when it becomes a major personnel issue and the pastor realizes, almost too late, that he has people who are misfits. At that point, relationships could be worked on with perhaps a happier solution. If the pastor, in tandem with a personnel committee, conducted a six-month review and an annual evaluation that included complete performance and compensation review, this would be a significant step toward building healthy working relationships. In the six-month review, the pastor could point out to the staff person the areas that need work and then monitor the progress. At the annual review, if there is no change, that may be the time for the pastor to point out that the association is not working out. After this type of discussion, the associate may want to search for another church.

In preparing for a review, it is appropriate to ask the employee to respond in advance to some questions, such as: What have you accomplished in ministry during the past six months? What do you plan to accomplish in the next six months? How can I, as head of staff, be more helpful to you in your ministry? What are you doing currently to build your own spiritual life (books you are reading, courses you are studying, etc.)? In what area can I be praying for you?

Well-documented reviews are the best tools to affirm good work and to call people to accountability. Unfortunately, pastors are not in the habit of keeping good records. Being nonconfrontive in nature, they often avoid dealing with the difficult issues until they are backed into a corner. Then they come out swinging at everyone and everything.

As the tension grows, the congregation has become aware of the problem. When the associate leaves, the people who loved him ask, "Why did the pastor push him out?" The people who are glad to see the associate go say, "Why did it take the pastor so long to get rid of this person? He should have been gone years ago." The pastor catches all the flack and recoils from the barrage coming from the congregation. Once he puts himself back together, he begins again to reach out to bring healing to the congregation, redefine the role, find another person, and start all over again. The time lag in productivity can cost a church several years. It takes only one personnel problem to cause a church to limp in ministry for three to five years.

VACATION, STUDY LEAVE, OR SABBATICAL

Pastors are generally given a four-week vacation and a two-week study leave. Larger churches and length of service may extend these terms.

Many churches prefer that the pastor take his vacation and study leave a week or two at a time, rather than all at once. It is clearly understandable that the congregation doesn't want to be without their pastor for an extended period. After all, what if Uncle Harry died?!

A week here and there is not enough time for a pastor to detach from his work and become refreshed, renewed, and recharged for ministry. When the restorative process is just beginning, it is time to pack up and get back to work.

Many pastors who take vacation one week at a

time eventually are burned out by mid-ministry. They have sacrificed so much of themselves for the congregation that they become physically and spiritually spent. At this point, some pastors leave the ministry, change churches, or take a sabbatical. Those are not always positive steps. Sometimes leaving the ministry is the church's loss and another profession's gain. Sometimes changing churches is like putting a Band-Aid on a broken leg: it covers up the wound, but doesn't heal the break. Sometimes a sabbatical can bring new meaning and direction to a pastor's ministry.

Unfortunately, many pastors return from a six- or twelve-month sabbatical and find their church has gone on without them. Seldom are they able to recapture the heart of the congregation as before the leave. Or during the sabbatical the pastor's view of ministry changes dramatically and it no longer fits the congregation back home.

A reasonable alternative would be for pastors to use all their vacation at once, and perhaps split the study time into two periods. This will provide three distinct times during the year when a pastor can pause to be renewed.

EXECUTIVE PASTOR

When a church reaches a size where two thousand or more attend worship regularly, when the senior pastor's ministry carries him beyond the local congregation (travel, seminary teaching, writing, media work, and so forth), or when the ministry reaches a size that requires a great deal of administrative time, calling an executive pastor could be the answer to an administrative headache. Megachurches are moving more and more in this direction.

An executive pastor, generally, is second in the chain of command. The staff reports to the senior pastor through the executive. The executive pastor must oversee the day-to-day programmatic operation of the church. When a church reaches this size, a full-time business administrator oversees the plant, budget, and personnel. The executive pastor sees that facilities are running on track, administers programs, and deals with staff development, long-range planning, publications, and public relations. The executive pastor assumes the role of running the church without preaching on Sunday morning or moderating monthly board meetings.

The key to this concept's success is that the senior pastor must delegate not only full responsibility to the executive pastor, but also full authority to get the job done. This is easier said than done. The senior pastor may delegate successfully at peak pressure times, but when the pressure is lessened he feels the need to manage the church more closely, and slowly begins to take back what he had readily given up before. There begins the creative tension between executive pastor and the senior pastor.

A REASONABLE ALTERNATIVE

Though this may be a workable model in a megachurch, it does not work in a smaller setting. Usually a budget prevents it and there is not enough work to warrant it. Unfortunately, the model becomes very attractive to pastors in smaller churches. When the day-to-day administrative work becomes a chore and a bore, the senior pastor believes the only solution is an executive pastor to whom he can delegate unpleasant tasks. For those pastors, there is a reasonable alternative.

In a small church with small staff and program, the pastor oversees it all. When the church grows to a place of three hundred regular worshipers, the pastor's secretary takes on some of the administrative work.

As the church grows to six hundred worshipers, the pastor's secretary can no longer do his secretarial work and all the administrative work. The solution is to hire someone part-time to relieve the clerical load. The pastor's secretary then functions as a church administrator or office manager.

By the time nine hundred people are worshiping, there is a definite need for a full-time business administrator with management expertise to supervise the organizational operation of the church. This person plans and administers the budget; manages personnel; sees to the maintenance and repair of facilities; oversees insurance, employee benefits, and investments; acts as a liaison with the community; and works with architects and contractors in renovating facilities. At this point the church administrator or office manager is phased out because the work has been placed in the position description of the business administrator. The programmatic administration goes back to the pastor's administrative assistant.

As the attendance reaches twelve hundred, the staff and program will require someone to coordinate the effort of the church. The administrative assistant has all she can do to keep up with her energetic boss. This is about the time the senior pastor begins to think he could use an executive pastor, like he has heard about in the big churches. Instead, he should employ someone who would merely coordinate the programmatic effort of the church. A lay person with programmatic administrative gifts could see to scheduling, forward planning, communication, and publicity just as an executive pastor would, but without pastoral or supervisory responsibilities. This person would be directly accountable to the senior pastor and would work with him in implementing his vision and direction for the church. An employee fitting this description would be less of a threat to the senior pastor, could be hired quickly without a lengthy search process, and would relieve the senior pastor of the administrative chores that bog him down.

THE TRUE TEST

The hard-driving nature of a senior pastor will sometimes draw criticism from staff and congregation. He can be thought of as ruthless, unfair, hungry for success, powerful, manipulative, and intimidating. In some instances, all of these things are true. But more often his actions are misunderstood. Ultimately, the senior pastor must live with his actions each day. If he truly believes he has made the right decisions, he will continue to move forward in a fruitful ministry. But if he knows that he has manipulated someone, undercut a staff member, or failed to give someone a chance, he will live with that unrest until it is resolved.

> *The man's no bigger than the way*
> *He treats his fellow man;*
> *This standard has his measure been*
> *Since time itself began!*
>
> *He's measured not by tithes or creed*
> *High-sounding though they be;*
> *Not by the bold that's put aside;*
> *Not by his sanctity;*

He's measured not by social rank,
When character's the test;
Nor by his earthly pomp or show,
Displaying wealth possessed!

He's measured by his justice, right,
His fairness at his play,
His squareness in all dealings made,
His honest, upright way.

These are his measures, ever near
To serve him when they can;
For man's no bigger than the way
He treats his fellow man!

—Unknown

CHAPTER 10

RUNNING IN THE SHADOW

"Let us run with endurance the race that is set before us, looking unto Jesus, the author and finisher of our faith, who for the joy that was set before Him endured the cross, despising the shame, and has sat down at the right hand of the throne of God. For consider Him who endured such hostility from sinners against Himself, lest you become weary and discouraged in your souls."

—*Hebrews 12:1–3*

ASSOCIATE OR ASSISTANT PASTORS

Most associate pastors are on their way somewhere else. Very few associate or assistant pastors go to a church with the idea they will always be an assistant or an associate in ministry. Ultimately their dream is to pastor their own church. When an associate does his job effectively, the congregation wants to see him stay. Eventually, however, the associate outgrows his role at that particular church and it becomes clear that God is calling him to a new ministry somewhere else.

The role of an associate is an important one in the life of a large church. An associate touches members of the congregation that the senior pastor will never reach. Often intimidated by a senior pastor, a parishioner will look to an associate for counsel, guidance, and direction. An associate has an extremely fruitful ministry because of his availability and person-to-person contact. There is nothing that pleases a senior pastor more than to know an associate is ministering to those people in the church family that he cannot reach.

Sharing ministry through preaching, communion, baptisms, weddings, and funerals is another very important function of an associate.

Once the challenge goes out of ministry, it is usually a clear indication that the Lord is calling the associate to go on to something new. When the associate has served about five years in a church, he reaches the point of career maturity and some restlessness begins. He will begin to maneuver for position, not always deliberately, and he will sometimes feel he has the right to tell the senior pastor what to do and how to do it. A power struggle develops between the head of staff and the associate. Why is this? The associate desires to grow further, and the only way to do that is to grow right into the senior pastor's territory. That is where conflict begins. When the associate realizes it is time to move on, it may take a year or two before he receives the call to another church. During this time there may be constant creative tension between the pastor and that associate. They are both struggling for the same position of leadership. By the time the associate has moved on, the relationship can be quite strained.

Chuck was a bright, young associate only two or three years out of seminary. He had been called to a good position at a church which had been pastored by the same man for about twelve years. The first year for Chuck was exciting, and he was learning what ministry was all about. By the middle of the second year, he had many questions about why they were doing things the way they were, and he wondered if they could try things a different way. He shared with me his concerns about the head of staff and his failure to understand things the way Chuck saw them. Chuck thought they should be moving much faster than they were.

When Chuck was into his fourth year, his frustration level prompted him to begin the search for a call to a new church. He received a call as associate to a church three times the size of his first church. Ministry took on a whole new look. It was a challenge, to say the least. Programs had to be developed, committees dealt with, and there was little time to pastor people.

About six months into his new position, he wrote to his former boss and said he had never realized what a head of staff goes through until then. He apologized if he caused him upset or frustration and thanked him for his patience and understanding. Even then, though, he could see how things could be improved in his new setting, if the senior pastor would just get with it. The senior pastor had more than thirty years experience on Chuck, and fifteen years in that church to build ministry.

Two or so years into this position, Chuck was

wooed away again as an associate to a church about three times the size of the second one. I talked with him about six months after his move. He said it had not been easy. One of the biggest lessons he had learned in ministering in a megachurch is that associates care for people by programming to meet their needs rather than through one-to-one pastoral ministry. Though some of that was prevalent in the first church, his primary ministry was one-to-one contact with the people. He praised his two former bosses, and he fondly remembered his first days in ministry. The frustration and upset that he voiced to me so long ago have faded into the past.

The relationship Chuck has with his first boss is solid and strong and healthy. When some associates part company with the senior pastor, the strain in the relationship is so great that it simply is never repaired.

Some heads of staff feel rejected when an associate leaves whether the senior pastor wants him to leave or not. The senior pastor says, "Well, another one has bailed out on me. He's gone off to do another job in another church. He had a big piece of my life. He has been helping me keep this machine going, and now I have to stop what I'm doing and try to keep it all together. He has turned his back on me." This feeling prompts the pastor to shut that person out of his life.

The associate may not feel that way at all. Instead, he may be appreciative of the way the senior pastor encouraged him, taught him, and allowed him to develop ministry. Unfortunately, the former associate can't reestablish a relationship with him because the head of staff thinks he has been rejected and has burned the bridge of communication.

What so many heads of staff fail to see is that they have been successful one more time, launching yet another person into ministry. The big churches with multiple staffs are the training grounds for pastors. The smaller churches watch the big ones and call pastors from them because of the training and the experience they have received. Instead of feeling rejected, the senior pastor ought to praise the Lord and acknowledge that an associate has been called to another pulpit. He should trust that all of what has been learned as a staff member will help in the ministry that God has given him.

MAINTAINING THE PACE

We have already discussed that senior pastors who have reasonably large staffs are visionaries and workaholics. Perhaps those very characteristics have brought them to churches of larger size and more complex ministry. *They sometimes fail to realize that they run so far ahead of their own staffs, they tend to leave them in the dust.*

A workaholic usually has high expectations of the people around him as well as of himself. Those high expectations are rarely met. The pastor, though appreciative of everything people do, communicates somehow that one hasn't done the job well enough. Staff members, then, run a race that is not designed for them. They are trying to run at the same pace the head of staff is running, even though they are cut out to run a different kind of race.

When a pastor of a large church is looking for staff, he wants productive people with high energy. The staff members, though highly energetic, cannot run at the same pace as the head of staff. Though staff members are running at their full strength, they feel they need to be running with the head of staff. In trying to step up to his pace, they find they simply cannot make it over the long haul. They maintain the pace for a brief period, but not for an extended period of time. *The head of staff will dream another dream and stride off leaving the staff member exhausted in his dust.*

Eventually staff members burn out or realize they can no longer keep up, and they slow the pace of their ministry. The head of staff, striding ahead by leaps and bounds, will not understand why his team isn't with him. Seldom does he slow down, allowing them to catch up.

If the head of staff is a visionary, this pattern is consistent in churches of all sizes. In an hour of quiet thinking, a visionary can generate enough ideas that could keep many people busy for months. It takes him only an hour to conceive the dream, but it could take his entire staff a great deal of time to carry it out. Unfortunately, the visionary does not always realize that it takes time to bring dreams to reality. "Why, it only took an hour for me to think of it, why is it taking so much time for all of these people to produce it?" While they work hard to make this dream a reality, he is already dreaming of new ideas.

HOLDING FORTH THE VISION TOGETHER

Often the senior pastor fails to include his people in the creative process. If he brought the staff into the process and they explored the possibilities of a new program together, shared vision and ownership could take place. The pastor would then delegate plans to staff members for implementation and check periodically to see that the work is being done.

Visionaries are not detail oriented and will sometimes fail to carry the vision all the way to the people. Visionaries will dream the dream and talk about it in staff meeting. The staff will take the dream to committees. The committees will talk about the dream and bring it back to staff. The staff will talk about the dream some more. Then the staff will decide the dream needs to go to the board. By then it could be three months or more since the pastor dreamed his dream. He is already thinking of new ideas, believing that this dream is well on its way to fruition. By the time it goes before the elder board and the leadership, however, the dream is already diluted in strength because the senior pastor has turned his energy to a new effort. The dream may meet with halfhearted response and pass the board, but now it limps out to the congregation, instead of moving to the congregation with great enthusiasm and gusto.

In his enthusiasm to be about new things, many of the really good things that the pastor has envisioned for the church are sometimes greatly diluted or left in the dust, because he has not slowed down long enough to develop his visions to get them to a place where they will eventually stand alone.

What about the pastor who limits the staff? He wants to launch his dreams with the same number of staff, and he will not provide for any additional help in facilitating the dream. That's another way of killing staff. If a staff is really working at maximum effectiveness, and the pastor continues to give them more work, he is responsible for burning them out. He fails to recognize that some of the people on his staff do not share his level of energy.

In 1972, Dr. Lloyd Ogilvie presented the elders of

the First Presbyterian Church of Hollywood with a call to commitment paper. This paper shared his view of ministry for the coming years. I believe it applies not just to the church in Hollywood but to the church at large. He wrote, *"The essential, undergirding direction is that professional staff exist to enable the people in ministry and not to do the ministry for people. The goal is deployment in the world, not just a church program. The church as an equipping center, a deployment agency for evangelism and mission, a healing community and a worshiping congregation provides the basis for staff needs."*

If that is true, and if a pastor has that type of philosophy, the program staff must take those dreams and reproduce them in the lives of the laypeople of the congregation. They must learn to duplicate themselves so that the laypeople begin to generate some of the program that is envisioned for the church. It should not all rest in the hands of a few paid staff members. This breaks down when staff people don't know how to let go of a project or program. Afraid that it will fail, staff members tend to do it themselves or work with a committee to carry out the project. By doing this, they are limiting how much can be done for the Lord in that church.

SUPPORTING THE MINISTRY

We lean toward staffing our churches with program people, associates, and qualified professional laypeople to do a variety of ministry in the church. Many churches fail to build a support staff that will help them complete that work. We are limiting how much those professionals can do because they get bogged down with placing their own phone calls and performing clerical chores that someone else could do for them. If the church could provide adequate secretarial or technical assistance, the staff would be able to accomplish more in the long run.

Often staff members become so caught up in ministry that they gradually become exhausted, burned out and, in some cases, spiritually spent. Because of the pace and demands on their life, they will sometimes sacrifice their family life and spiritual life. A time to get away and be quiet and hear what God would have for them would be beneficial, but times like those grow fewer in number because of the expanding ministry that has been placed upon them. Many associates find themselves in a psychologist's office saying, "What is wrong with me? I feel like I am falling apart." Others will take a call to another church to get away from the pressure. (That provides only temporary relief, until the pressure builds in the new location.) Another group of people turn their backs on the ministry and move into another career because they can't take the pressure. Many of them struggle with high blood pressure, ulcers, and other stress-related illnesses that are so prevalent today. When everything is reviewed and considered, the very core of the problem is that they were forced to run a race at a pace that was not meant for them.

How do you prevent that from happening? A senior pastor who is a caring, compassionate man of God, who throws his arms around the congregation on Sunday morning, who loves, affirms, and appreciates them, sometimes fails to do that with his staff. He doesn't recognize signs of weariness, stress, overload, and burnout. He expects the job to be done. If, instead, the head of staff would step back far enough to recognize what is happening, he might say, "My God, what am I doing to my staff? How can I help them get the job done?" If he could see that providing temporary help for the staff would get them over the rough spots, and through a certain period of the year when programming is tough, it could contribute to the health and well-being of a staff. It might mean temporary assistance in the business office to get the stewardship program together or to close the books at the year's end. It might mean recruiting several good volunteers to do clerical work, run errands, stock curriculum, or dress bulletin boards. When there is overload and the regular secretarial assistance is not enough, temporary assistance can be a lifesaver.

Interns from a local seminary make good program assistants and do an excellent job of relieving overload work. The learning experience prepares them for what they will eventually face in ministry. It is good training and provides a tremendous service to the church.

Churches talk often about developing the volunteer forces in the church. Pastors say they would like to have a director of volunteers to enlist people to do some of the overload work. We do need to implement our volunteers, but what many pastors fail to realize is that most of the volunteer force for the last fifty years has been women. Those women have gone into the work force. Instead of volunteering their services, they are getting paid for their efforts. It has reduced the volunteer potential in our country to a minimum. The ones that are available are either retired senior citizens or, occasionally, young mothers. Both those groups carry certain limitations. Young mothers are only available at certain times. If their children become ill, they are not available at all. Retired folks are available when they want to be. They want the freedom to be able to travel and to enjoy the latter years of their life and don't want to be tied down to a regular responsibility. Some senior citizens are the first to volunteer, but they are no longer capable of doing the kind of work that needs to be done. It will often take more time and energy to round up volunteers to do a job, organize the task to be done, and teach them how to do it than for staff persons to do the job themselves.

With paid temporary help comes a certain level of professionalism and confidentiality. There are no guarantees with volunteers.

I am often asked if I recommend hiring staff from within the membership of the church. My answer is always yes. Many question me for that and say, "Why, what happens if the pastor's secretary is a member of the church and she just doesn't work out?" I respond with, "So you let her go!" "But, she is a member of the church," they will argue. Again, I say to them, "So you let her go!" *If you are careful about who you hire, you may not be in a position of having to fire.* They emphasize their position by pointing out that if the staff member is a member of the congregation and if they must handle matters that are confidential, they are fearful that the staff member will talk about it to their friends in the congregation. A nonmember can blab the word all over the community, and it will sift back to the membership of the church. It is all in finding trainable individuals who can be trusted and who are self-motivated, dependable, and loyal.

Many support staff who are members of the congregation struggle with where to place their loyalty. They are torn with being loyal to the congregation they have been a part of for twenty-five years or being loyal to the pastor for whom they work. Their primary loyalty must be to the person to whom they report, whether it is an associate on the staff or to the head of staff. Ultimately, their first loyalty is to the staff. They must recognize the fact that they are on the ground floor of future ministry and are privy to information the congregation is unaware of and should not be aware of until the appropriate time.

CONSENSUS MANAGEMENT LEADS TO CRISIS MANAGEMENT

Many churches function under crisis management because they are attempting to cope with the tyranny of the urgent. The "urgent" can manifest itself in a turnover of staff that leaves things somewhat disorganized. It can be a financial crisis that has facilitated a cutback in program and personnel. It can be a lot of little things that have gained strength and momentum over a period of time. Crisis management can place unfair pressure on an entire staff, and all but wear them out.

Crisis management and consensus management are directly connected; one feeds the other. To illustrate consensus management, many churches will call seminary graduates to serve as associates because the salary demands are not as great. Though there is much talk about "team effort" and "collegiality" in the staff, there is still a boss.

Consistently, I talk with associates in large churches around the country who believe they have the right to do ministry their way, regardless of what the head of staff may say. They develop an arrogance about their work. They become territorial of their ministry area and develop a defensive posture should anyone question their role. They become possessive of the people in their programs, on their committees, and under their supervision. This attitude forms a tunnel vision that is extremely destructive to a church.

When that happens, staff meetings become less productive as the jockeying for position takes place, and the associates insist that everyone make the decisions. The head of staff, wanting to keep peace and not seem dictatorial, slowly begins to bow to the pressure where literally everything that is brought up is questioned and not settled until there is consensus. If one or two staff members hold out and no decision on an issue is made, then the minority voice, in essence, has made the decision. I have seen associates or other professional staff members pout, make threats about leaving, or throw "adult tantrums" until they get their way.

Over a period of time, consensus management diminishes the strength, energy, and confidence of the head of staff until he wonders about his own effectiveness. During these times, the pastor will often take a sabbatical, pour himself into a project outside the church, or closet himself and write a book. At that point, crisis management takes over.

Ultimately, when the head of staff becomes fully aware of what has been happening to him, he usually makes a conscious decision to regain the pastoral leadership of his church and assert himself more fully in an effort to reestablish his leadership. When he takes these steps, the program staff develops an attitude problem and low morale. Then stories are told from church to church about how difficult it is to work on the staff at that church.

In my opinion, seminaries do not prepare their students for ministry in megachurches by teaching them how to be accountable and subordinate to a head of staff. When a church has two pastors, to work together in consensus is often healthy and harmonious. However, when a church has many pastors, trying to get consensus among all of them can bring a church to a standstill.

"We have met the enemy and he is us!" (Pogo).

CHAPTER 11

FROM RUNNING IN DESPAIR TO STRIDING IN VICTORY

"The Lord heals not for our comfort, but for His mission!"

—Lloyd Ogilvie

I made my way through the jetway of the airport and scanned the crowd for Cal's face. Cal pastors a large church and I had spent time with his staff a number of months earlier helping them to be more effective in the ministry to which God had called them. Our eyes met, we exchanged hugs, he took my bag, and we headed out of the airport.

When I asked "How are you?" he responded,

"Carolyn, I've never been so discouraged in twenty-five years of ministry!" During the hours that followed, he shared with me all the pain, frustration, disappointment, stress, and discouragement of pastoral ministry.

Just a few months earlier, everything seemed positive, and now the bottom had fallen out of ministry for this pastor. It seemed that everything Cal put his hand and heart to didn't work.

He shared with me the unrest in his congregation: how some folks wanted him to preach more evangelical sermons and others wanted him to preach to the social needs. Some of his people had become apathetic pew-sitters who showed up on Sunday morning out of duty and were not willing to be involved in the life of the church. Others were on fire to pull the church out of the denomination because they were unhappy with some recent stands the church had taken. Cal was faced with trying to bring healing in order to prevent a split in his congregation.

He shared with me the frustration of trying to lead a staff that did not share the same sense of direction for ministry. They did their job, but they just didn't seem to function as a team. There was unrest and conflict. Cal knew some changes needed to be made, but he was fearful of rocking the boat and making matters worse.

As the hours passed, I thought surely there must be an end to all this. But as that very thought was going through my mind, Cal began to share how his own spiritual life had dried up. He was finding it more and more difficult to prepare sermons. His prayer life had withered, too.

I knew he was finally coming to the end of his story

when he said, "If something doesn't happen to change all this, I'm going to leave the ministry."

Discouragement and its two sidekicks, stress and burnout, are running rampant through ministry today. Cal's story was similar to many others I had heard during the past year. Discouragement tackles all of us from time to time, no matter what role we fill on the staff of a church. It is the primary reason for pastors leaving the ministry. Burnout strikes associate pastors, youth directors, administrators, lay professionals, and clerical personnel.

Why does it happen? Why does it take its toll the way it does? Why don't we recognize it until we become almost totally helpless? I believe that discouragement takes hold so gradually over a period of time that we are not aware of it until it has brought us to the breaking point.

More than thirty years ago, in a crowded dining hall at the Forest Home Christian Conference Center, I heard the still, small voice of God and gave my life to Him. Over those many years, there have been mountaintop experiences and great growth. There have been times of living on a plateau and occasionally a few low times. I've had a remarkable thirty years filled with great joy and victory as a Christian.

My spiritual life took root and grew as a result of the ministry of the First Presbyterian Church of Hollywood. That great church has stood the test of time. As a result of the faithfulness to the call of ministry, lives have been changed, ministries launched, pastors trained, and laypersons equipped with the gospel in such a way that they have developed a reproductive faith.

After fifteen years of volunteer ministry, I became

a part of the staff of my church. At first it was a part-time support position, but after several years it developed into a full-time position coordinating much of the program. It was the last five years of my tenure that equipped me to respond to Cal and to minister to so many discouraged people today. During that time I was stretched to my limit and possibly beyond. My mind was challenged, and I grew beyond my own understanding. I was a layperson with a practical, pew-gained theology. I didn't know at the time that God had not only drawn me to this position, but had given me the gifts to do the work. Those gifts were molded on God's anvil and it is only now, many years later, that I can honestly identify and claim them as having come from God.

It was an awesome experience for me to work closely with some of the great minds of the church. To share my ideas with them and help them develop programs that would meet the needs of our people was a real adventure, and it called forth the best in me. What a joy it was to know that I had been a small part of a program that was instrumental in changing people's lives.

Having been placed in a position of leadership, I gradually assumed more and more of what needed to be done because there was no one else to do it. There were pressures, frustrations, and feelings of being pulled in many different directions. But all this was smoothed over by the love of Christ, the call to commitment, and the knowledge that I was doing this to God's glory.

THE DRYING-UP PROCESS

Over the course of many long months, the seeds of discouragement, stress, and burnout struggled to take root deep within me. I can't even tell how or when it happened. It just did.

All the spiritual growth and input accumulated over the years, all the conferences and retreats, all the independent study, all the learn-from-experience elements of faith just slowly dried up. Sunday morning worship services became time for me to check out who was sitting with whom, look at people's new clothes, and notice when the organist missed a cue. And yet when I saw our dear pastor the next week, I found myself telling him what a great message he gave on Sunday, knowing I had heard very little. The joy of going to work at the church slowly ebbed. I had been putting out so much for so long, I had no more resources to draw from.

My Bible reading became less frequent and prayer times more brief. Eventually I reached a point where I felt there was nothing to pray for. *I never doubted God, nor His saving power, I just ceased to tap it.*

Then a staff retreat came around. I made all the arrangements for it and scheduled it to be held at Forest Home, the very place where my spiritual life began. When the day came and I began to drive to the retreat, I wondered why I was even going. What did I have to offer? I surely expected absolutely nothing from it.

Following dinner, we gathered for a time of Bible study and caring and praying for one another. As I listened to my brothers and sisters share their needs, I suddenly realized that I had touched rock bottom. I was spent, used up, burned out! Sitting there quietly and tearfully, my first thought was to panic and run from this group who had become my family. How could I ever begin to tell them what had been happening to me? What would happen to my credibility if I shared my pain with them? Whatever would they say if they knew that I was the weak link in the chain? I couldn't say a word. I thought I would just sit quietly and try to ignore the pain.

OUT OF THE DARKNESS
AND INTO THE LIGHT

We had progressed into a prayer time of individuals praying for one another as the Spirit would lead. I had no inclination to pray for anyone. Besides, everyone was doing so well without me. It was not long before the inevitable thing happened. Everyone had sought prayer except me. I had a decision to make. Should I continue to sit quietly and hope that no one would notice that I had not been a part of the prayer circle and had not sought prayer for myself?

Sometimes when we have ignored God's gentle prodding, He grabs us and propels us to where He wants us to be. That's what He did to me. Before I knew it, I was placed before Him seeking the prayers of my brothers and sisters. Three members of the staff whom I love dearly, and who have had strategic roles in my life, immediately gathered around me and prayed for me. I don't think they had a clue to my condition, but with their prayers they lifted my broken state before the Almighty and I could actually feel a healing process begin to take place.

It was incredible! I felt as though a great earthquake were going on inside of me. One of the hands that was laid on me trembled as the healing power came through to me. Then in a moment the trembling was stilled, and in its place was a very great peace and serenity and a feeling of beginning again.

The next morning dawned bright and beautiful

and we gathered in the clear, crisp air to worship. As the Spirit led, we shared Scripture verses or hymns. I sat there bathing in the warm sunshine, drinking in all the verses shared. There wasn't one that I had not memorized at some time in my life, and yet each one came alive as if it were the first time I had heard it. My heart was filled with the profound but childish hymn, "Jesus Loves Me." I really had gone back to the beginning. At last, the Lord gave me a verse to share— "The Lord is my Shepherd, I shall not want." That was brief, and to the point, but I had managed to say something. *As I spoke the words, I realized once again that my Lord would supply my every need and that He would carry me in my weariness.*

On Sunday I went to church and did all the usual things that are expected of me on a Sunday, but I also worshiped. Our pastor spoke that portion of Psalm 17 that says, "Keep me as the apple of Your eye; Hide me under the shadow of Your wings," and then "As for me, I will see Your face in righteousness; I shall be satisfied when I awake in Your likeness." Imagine me being the "apple of His eye!" Of course, why not? He had been reassuring me of His love over the past days.

The next Sunday's text came booming forth from our pastor, "The Lord is my Shepherd, I shall not want." And on through the entire psalm. How could my pastor have known months ago when he prepared this sermon series that God would use this with such impact on a staff member? He didn't know, but God did!

And so it was out of the depths of discouragement and despair that God lifted me to new heights. I was on my way once again. The Scriptures came alive, my prayers took focus and had meaning, and I charged ahead in my work without ever sharing with another person what I had come through.

More than a year passed, and the intensity and the volume of my work increased. But when a doctor informed me that I had a stress-related illness, I knew that I had some decisions to make. Should I continue working? Or should I resign in an effort to regain my health? How do you just walk away from something that has been so much a part of your life for so many years? Could I leave the position and be content with being a member of the congregation? As I wrestled with those questions, God made it clear to me that I had said and done all I could and that it was time to resign.

A PART OF HIS PLAN

Having taken that step, my plan was to return to being Mrs. Happy Homemaker, but that was not God's plan. Within a few short months, He made it clear to me that He did not want me to stay home. He had placed me in a position where I learned the work of the church from the bottom up and the heart and soul of pastoral ministry from some of the best in our land. He had equipped me for ministry.

And now, a number of years later, I reflect on what I experienced, and I recognize the tremendous growth that came from pain. *When I got serious with God, He opened the doors to a ministry that is beyond anything I could humanly conceive.* He has taken me all over the country. He has paved the way and developed a ministry that calls forth all the spiritual gifts He has given me.

By running in the shadow, always trying to measure up, and trying to maintain someone else's pace, I found I was running in despair. *His profound touch on my life has turned that running into a striding with Him.* To stride is to achieve the most effective natural pace; maximum competence or capability. The days may be long, the work challenging, but they fit the stride that He has given to me.

As I listened to Cal share his discouragement, I honestly knew what he was experiencing and was grateful that he at least had the courage to talk about it to someone. Just verbalizing the pain sometimes relieves the pressure enough so that we can begin again.

Coping with discouragement requires looking into the core of our very being. If the spiritual wellspring from which we feed has dried up, then the first step is to get in step with God again. Coming out of discouragement and stress takes time, just as it took time to fall so far down. But with persistent effort it is possible to come back. The beautiful part of it is that the new person we become as a result of all our experience is someone very special.

In this ministry that God has given me, there are times when I have the awesome pleasure of watching the power of the Holy Spirit at work. When I come alongside a discouraged pastor for a few days and help him find a way out of a dilemma, I often stand aside and become a spectator of the healing power of God. More than once, I have found myself crying out to God, "What have I done to deserve witnessing all of this? Why me, God?" And He consistently responds, "Why not you?"

> *When things go wrong as they sometimes will,*
> *When the road you're trudging seems all uphill,*
> *When the funds are low and the debts are high,*

And you want to smile, but you have to sigh,
When care is pressing you down a bit,
Rest, if you must, but don't you quit.
Life is queer with its twists and turns,
As everyone of us sometimes learns,
And many a failure turns about,
When we might have won had we stuck it out;
Don't give up though the pace seems slow,
You may succeed with another blow.
Success is failure turned inside out,
The silver tint of the clouds of doubt,
And you can never tell how close you are,
It may be near when it seems so far;
So stick to the fight when you're hardest hit,
It's when things seem worst that you must not quit.
                              —Unknown

CHAPTER 12

THE PERFECT MATCH

---◆---

"For God so loved the world, He did not send a committee!"

One warm summer morning, I received a call from a member of a pastor search committee for a large church in Southern California. This church was looking for an associate pastor, and my name had been given as a reference for a particular candidate.

After identifying herself, the committee member asked, "Do you think this fellow could do the job?"

"What is the job?" I responded.

"Well, it's a . . . well, the senior pastor is going to take a sabbatical during the summer and so this person would have to preach, but then he probably would not have many opportunities to do that throughout the year. He would do some worship planning and . . . we're very flexible. We're hoping to fill several positions in the next couple of years, so, well, you know, he could do most anything."

Though I was somewhat familiar with the size and location of the church, I certainly had no information about its style, its leadership, or its direction, and I told her I simply could not make a clear recommendation based on what she had told me.

I inquired about a position description. Had one been written?

"Well, no, not really," came the response.

I suggested that the position had been defined on the paperwork that went to the denominational headquarters that initiated the position.

"Oh, yes," came the reply. "Would you like me to read it to you?"

I thought that might be helpful. There was a long pause at the other end of the line, while the caller searched for the paperwork. She came back to the phone, somewhat exasperated and said, "I can't find that paperwork right now. Honestly, we just want someone who can do the job."

I could hear the frustration in her voice and attempted to help her focus on some specifics. "Do you need someone to do youth work?"

"No, we have that," she said.

"Do you want someone to do children's ministry?"

"No, we have that, too."

"Do you want someone to do administrative work?"

"Well, no, we have that also."

The next question hit the jackpot. "Do you want someone to do adult education, counseling, membership development, Stephens Ministry, evangelism, or mission?"

"Oh," she responded excitedly, "yes, yes, yes! We need someone to do all of those things. That's it. That's the position we are trying to fill."

In a church the size of the one she was representing, it would take two or three associates or lay professionals to do that job.

This is not an unusual illustration. Many churches today form a committee to search for someone to fill a vacancy, but they don't know what they're looking for. In some denominations, a search committee is formed by an elective process of the congregation. It is meant to be representative of the congregation, but in actuality "the squeaky wheel gets the grease." *The group of people who are the most vocal and most influential about what they perceive to be the direction of the church will often gain control of the committee.* This faction usually surfaces out of a reaction to some things that have gone on in the previous pastorate in the church, rather than in response to what has happened positively in the church.

For instance, for a period of years a church may have had a primarily conservative/traditionalist pastor. When he leaves, certain members who feel they need someone who is more evangelical may make their voice heard. This rather small group of people will see that enough members of the search committee are evangelical in their stance. When it comes time to interview candidates, they look for evangelicals. They will tell a candidate that the congregation is very evangelical and will introduce the candidate to members who feel the same way.

If the candidate is an evangelical, he begins to dream of the wonderful ministry that will take place, and how exciting it will be to invite people to come to Christ at the close of the worship service. He envisions saving souls for Christ in this church. After all, everyone he has met wants this type of ministry.

Unfortunately, when he arrives, he finds that the

evangelical remnant is not as large as he understood it to be; the very thought of an evangelistic strategy shakes the pillars of the church. Within days of his arrival, he is forced to change his style of ministry if he is to survive in this pastorate. The conservative/ traditionalist members are expecting the new pastor to be just like Pastor Jones, others are hoping for someone who is more community-minded, and others are expecting a pastor in the charismatic vein, and on and on.

Is this a good match or a mismatch? Only time will tell. If the pastor is versatile, flexible, and capable of winning people to Christ by loving them, he may survive and the church may do reasonably well. If the pastor is not sensitive to some of these concerns and does not win the heart of the congregation, he will have a difficult time, and if he is not accepted by the congregation his tenure could be very brief.

Why does this scenario happen so often in the church? We can theorize about a great many things, but the answer to the question is poor communication. *Search committees simply don't know the questions to ask of a candidate, nor do they have a clear understanding of the direction of the church.* If the individuals of the committee don't know who they are spiritually and who the congregation is from a spiritual and theological perspective, they have no basis from which to evaluate the candidate. If the committee cannot articulate their faith and understand the doctrine and polity of their denomination and congregation, they have no way of knowing whether the answers the candidate may give are the correct answers for their church. A candidate can theologize in his most pastoral manner and sound very impressive to a committee. But if his theology is not the same as theirs, the committee must be astute enough to recognize that.

Interviewing a candidate begins when the committee reads his dossier or a letter of introduction. The candidate often does himself a disservice because he does not explain clearly enough who he is and what he believes in the dossier. Unfortunately, many candidates do not communicate clearly what their style and ministry are all about. During an interview, unless the committee is very spiritually discerning and has a good understanding of the theology of their congregation, they will not know the kind of questions to ask the candidate and will not know how to respond to the answers given.

During the interview process, there is a tendency on the part of the committee to look as good as possible. Candidates and their families will be taken to the nicest of restaurants and entertained in the homes of the most affluent people in the church. The committee often embellishes facts and figures because they are excited about who they are as a church. Search committees of some of the most troubled churches seldom recognize internal problems and think of themselves as a prime choice. They believe pastors ought to be begging for the call to serve their congregation. Unfortunately, they fail to recognize that conflict from a former pastorate, denominational dissatisfaction, consistent loss of membership, and a congregational split, are not what attracts a new pastor. A search committee will avoid discussing these problems in an effort to deny that this is part of who they are.

The perfect match occurs when the candidate writes a resume that reflects who he is in the sight of God, and the search committee is willing to be led by the power of the Holy Spirit. The ideal committee comprises people who are spiritual leaders of the church, the ones who show the greatest spiritual depth and understanding of what that church is theologically. When that combination of candidate and committee come together, they find they can be honest with each other about the church's strengths and weaknesses and the candidate's strengths and weaknesses. That is the beginning of building a real and honest relationship with each other. Even during the interview they can feel the freedom to care for one another and to pray together as a small community of the body of Christ. Then the chances are very good that this will be a perfect match and that ministry will move forward and be successful.

FORMING THE COMMITTEE

How do we form such a perfect committee? In a time of prayer, the church leaders need to seek God's guidance in selecting the right people to represent the congregation on this committee. It should represent the congregation in age, interest level, and areas in the church. It comprises people who know the congregation well and are spiritually discerning. Good candidates for the committee are people in the congregation who have some seminary background, who have done in-depth study in the Scriptures, or who have a good understanding of the denomination.

The committee should know the answers to their own questions and should understand religious vocabulary. If a committee asks a candidate if he is charismatic and he responds affirmatively, does that say to the committee that he speaks in tongues? Or does that say that anyone who believes in Jesus Christ is charismatic? If a candidate says he is a liberal, does that mean he's a Democrat? Or does that mean that his theology is liberal? And what about a candidate who volunteers that he is an evangelical but is not an evangelist? The committee must be astute enough to discern exactly what is being communicated. It may take a number of questions to understand where the candidate stands regarding a *charismatic* ministry, what he means by the word *liberal,* or how he can be an *evangelical* and not be an *evangelist.*

Instead of factions of the church being represented on a search committee, it would be well to have various parts of the body represented. The church is made up of a body of believers, and every congregation leans in a certain direction theologically and spiritually as to their view of the Scripture, the faith, the denomination, and so forth. There are some churches that are traditional, doctrinal, liturgical; some fundamental, conservative, or liberal; some evangelical, charismatic, or Pentecostal; and some with a mix of these. Many churches identify with one particular area. I believe that God calls us to be whole and complete people. Just as we have been given the Trinity (God the Father, the Son, and the Holy Spirit), all the aspects of who those three are should be found in the healthy, well-balanced church. God the Father sets down the laws and doctrines and the traditions of the church, regardless of denomination. In the Scriptures, He has given us the foundation of who we are as a church. God the Son, in Jesus Christ, the evangelical, came to show us how to share the good news of the gospel with other people. God the Holy Spirit is the personality, the charisma of the Trinity. It is the Holy Spirit who is the life breath in the church today and supplies all we need to live the Christian life.

If our local congregations are to be well-balanced,

all three of these aspects need to be functioning in harmony together. One should not be eliminated or one given more strength than the others. Parishioners who are shortsighted in their faith tend to bring a church out of balance because they will only focus on one or two of the aspects.

When a committee is composed of representatives of those three aspects that are united in doctrinal beliefs, share a vision for the future, and can be an objective thinking body, they will effectively communicate the soul of the congregation to the candidate. If a congregation contains all three aspects, it is imperative for the committee to seek a pastor who is skilled at maintaining the delicate balance and can build a strong ministry.

ASSOCIATE PASTORS

Most churches go through a lengthy process to select an associate pastor. If it has been a committee process and not left entirely in the hands of the senior pastor, it is important that the committee be in close contact with the senior pastor through the search process. When the list is narrowed to three or four candidates, the senior pastor ought to be involved directly in the choice of that final candidate and be allowed an unquestioned veto vote. Unfortunately, that isn't always the way it works out.

It is important that the senior pastor spend significant time with the candidate to see if they have a workable personality mix. The candidate may have every ability to do the task, but if his personality is not compatible with the senior pastor's, the relationship will never work. A one-hour interview with the pastor is not sufficient to know if they will be able to work together. A day together to learn how one another views ministry would be helpful. During that time, they should discover if one is open to facilitating the dream of the other, whether they can recognize what each other's role is and honor it, and if they can work within that structure. When the senior pastor comes to the search committee and says, "This is the person I believe I can work with and with whom I can build ministry," what was searched for has been found. This may not always be the candidate that the search committee had in mind. If so, it would be well for the search committee to spend additional time with the candidate in getting to know his heart and style of ministry, in an effort to better understand the decision of the senior pastor.

STAFF RESIGNATIONS

Probably the greatest gift a search committee could present to a new head of staff would be the written resignation of every member of the staff. The challenge of living with acquired staff is a very common complaint.

When the new head of staff arrives, he usually wants to communicate love and promote healing of any rifts that may have occurred before his arrival. One of the last things he wants to do is ask the staff to resign. So he will attempt to build ministry, somewhat shackled by a predesigned staff. One of the things that generally draws a search committee to a candidate is his style of ministry and what he has accomplished in other pastorates. To develop that type of ministry in his new setting, the pastor needs to be given the freedom to call and shape a staff that will facilitate that dream. A search committee may request a letter of resignation from each staff member, with the acceptance of that resignation to be determined within the first six months of the pastor's ministry. This period of time gives the pastor an opportunity to settle in, get acquainted, and determine if there are presently existing staff with whom he can comfortably work.

Often a pastor leaves a church because of difficult staff situations or because of conflict in staff. When this happens and a new pastor comes on the scene, he is often met with the same challenges as the former pastor. A staff that can't function together will not be any different when a new head of staff comes. If anything, the situation could get worse as they resist the authority and leadership of the new head of staff. This does not necessarily mean that the entire staff needs to move on. Sometimes it is just one or two people that keep everyone else stirred up and anxious.

If the search committee is reluctant to request resignations, the least it can do is to request the personnel committee to thoroughly evaluate every staff member. If there are problem people, the personnel committee should take steps to remedy the problem before the new pastor arrives.

Chuck and I sat in a coffee shop discussing staffing just three days before his installation service would take place. He resisted my words when I told him to ask for the resignation of every member of staff. He said he was comfortable working with all kinds of people, and this would be no problem. Four years later, he called to tell me he had resigned from the church, and that one of the most troublesome factors during his four years was that he had been shackled with an uncooperative and rebellious staff.

The search committee has a difficult task, but

with God, all things are possible. When a search committee fully understands what that means their lives are changed forever, and a pastor is called to minister to the flock they represent.

"Again I say to you that if two of you agree on earth concerning anything that they ask, it will be done for them by My Father in heaven. For where two or three are gathered together in My name, I am there in the midst of them" (Matt. 18:19–20).

CHAPTER 13

FAMILY IN THE FISHBOWL

"It is not who you are,
  but who you can be
  through Jesus Christ.
It is not where you are,
  but where you are
  going that counts.
It is not what you lack,
  but what you do with
  what you have that
  really makes the
  difference."
  —Unknown

I sat across the breakfast table from the pastor's wife on the first day of my visit to their church. As we talked over breakfast Barbara asked me, "How do you avoid pastoral leprosy?" I had not heard that phrase before and asked her to define it for me.

"Well, in the eyes of some of our congregation, the

pastor's family has leprosy. We are stared at from a distance—never excluded from an event, but never completely included. We hear shouts of criticism and few compliments. We are measured by a set of standards that are impossible to live up to. What is the cure for this?"

The pastor's family is set apart from the congregation; they are a family in a fishbowl. Every Sunday morning the congregation notices what the pastor's wife is wearing, whether she wore it last week, as well. They will notice whether her apparel is out of this season's Sears catalog or whether it came from Saks Fifth Avenue.

The same goes for the children of the pastor's family. They are expected to be perfect. Though members of the congregation will smile and lovingly chuckle if the children misbehave during worship service, they still say, "Can't that mother control her kids?" If the children run through the hallways or misbehave, people are reluctant to correct them. If they weren't the pastor's kids, everyone would get into the act of telling them what to do and what not to do. The pastor may be busy pastoring and the pastor's wife may be pouring coffee, unable to restrain her active youngsters. Yet people will stand by, watch, and criticize instead of lending a hand.

PIPELINE TO THE PASTOR

Often a pastor's wife is used as a vehicle to get to the pastor. People who don't have the courage to confront the pastor with a specific concern will casually drop by and visit with the pastor's wife. They will mention to her that they heard from someone else in the congregation that something is amiss. This, naturally, does not affect them, but they thought it would be good for the pastor's wife to know that this was going on. By communicating this concern to the pastor's wife, inevitably, over dinner that night the pastor is going to get the full story.

It is interesting, too, that the pastor can be on the firing line in the church. He can be heavily criticized about something he is doing or not doing, or about the direction the church is taking, and manage to deflect a lot of criticism and complaint. Additionally, he can turn his back on the gossip and walk away from some of the petty things that come before him, and, over all, he can be very forgiving of his congregation. However, what people don't realize is that as it rolls off the pastor, it rolls onto his wife. She becomes the receiver for the attacks on her husband. She loves him, and it hurts her to hear others attacking him.

Sadly, she has no one with whom she can share that hurt. If there is someone in the congregation, she risks having the word spread throughout the congregation again. If she shares her pain with a next-door neighbor or a friend in the PTA, she is saying that everything isn't wonderful in the church. That is not good publicity to those who are unchurched.

Sometimes a pastor's wife forms a bond with two or three women in the church who are stable, knowing she can share her pain in confidence. Others may have a trusted friend or counselor not connected with the church. Still others, having no one, hold it in and try to cope the best way possible.

FIRST FAMILY

In many churches, the pastor's family is considered the first family of the church. With that title, the congregation expects them to be and do far more than most families. They expect the children to be enthusiastic participants in the Sunday school program. Anything less than that, and they question whether the pastor is doing a good job in his own home.

The pastor's family is in a no-win situation no matter what they do. If he is a high-energy person who is deeply involved in his ministry as well as in community concerns and denominational matters, a pastor in a very large church generally has a strong wife who has a mind of her own and tends to be more verbal about what is going on in the church. Unless she holds that carefully, she can, in some instances, be a stumbling block for the pastor in his own ministry. She doesn't intend to do that, but in her enthusiasm and in her frustration at seeing things moving in a direction in which she is uncomfortable, she may assert herself in ways that can be viewed as less than positive. That is unfortunate because she means well. Some pastors' wives are extremely gifted women. They may have met while he was in seminary and while she was training for ministry as well. She brings wonderful gifts to the church. *The unfortunate thing is there are often instances where very gifted women are never given the opportunity in their own church to utilize their gifts the way they would be utilized if she were not the pastor's wife.*

In smaller churches, the pastor's wife will do the Christian education work but won't get paid for it. That is a real disservice to the family, too. The congregation is expecting two roles to be filled and is paying for only one. When that family leaves, the search committee may expect the new pastor's wife to run the education program because the former pastor's wife did.

They may be in for a real surprise when they discover she has no intention of running the Christian education program or even of teaching Sunday school.

THE MISTRESS

As we discussed in an earlier chapter, one of the loneliest careers is being a pastor, especially a head of staff. A lonelier role is to be a pastor's wife. Early in the ministry, as he becomes reasonably successful, he takes on a mistress. His wife soon realizes that the mistress gets far more of him than she does.

Every morning his wife kisses him good-by, and he goes off to his mistress who woos him and loves him, who affirms him and encourages him, who presents him with struggles and challenges, who stretches him beyond his limits, and who cheers for him when all is going well. Then he comes home weary after a very long day. He doesn't want to hear what the children have been doing, what happened at the PTA, that the plumbing is leaking, the lawn needs mowing, and a wife needs loving.

There comes a time in a pastor's life that he has to realize that his mistress is the church and that he is called to love his wife and to care for the church. He will maintain the right perspective and have the opportunity to be happy, with a happy family and congregation, if he can keep straight these priorities: who he is in the sight of God, who he is in his family's eyes, and finally who he is in the ministry.

Pastor or parishioner, we need to keep our relationship to the Lord in proper perspective. Next in order of importance comes our family, then our career, and then our life in the church and community. Pastors tend to rationalize these priorities by saying, "Well, who I am before God and my career are one and the same." When they do that, family is squeezed out because God and career become one. It is in walking the walk, the daily feeding and infilling from God, that the relationship to family is built and the nurture and care take place. This applies also to building the relationship in the congregation and helping the church family grow closer toward a living relationship with the Lord.

SUPERWOMAN

In the congregation's eyes, the pastor's wife is expected to be there whenever the church doors are open. It would be preferable, though physically impossible, for her to sing in the choir, teach Sunday school, pour coffee, attend a Sunday school class, work in the nursery, and sit in the third pew consistently during worship. (Incidentally, it doesn't matter where she sits in the sanctuary, she will sit alone unless she deliberately sits with someone. It matters not whether it is front or back, side or center, balcony or main floor, seldom will members come and join her in the pew.) Her attendance at a Sunday night service and a Wednesday night program is also expected. It goes almost without saying that she is expected to be an officer in the women's program. And if she is a caring person, she should be actively involved in some community effort.

What the congregation fails to realize is that today's woman, even the pastor's wife, is found more in the marketplace than at the kitchen sink. Pastors' wives are working in full-time positions and cannot give the time to work in the church as was once the pattern. It would be good for a congregation to accept and understand this and to offer encouragement, love, and affirmation to the pastor's wife for whatever her level of involvement. If it means that the only thing she can do is to have an open house for new members, the congregation needs to accept that. If they are critical of store-bought cookies, let a circle provide the dessert.

Sometimes a pastor's wife with extraordinary gifts in music, counseling, or education is not allowed to use them in her own church. Many wives have found fulfillment by utilizing their gifts and skills in another church. This is unfortunate, not only for the congregation, but also for the pastor and his wife as well.

A pastor's wife views her husband as a husband, and not as a pastor. She sees his flaws, she mends his socks, she sees him unshaven in all his humanity. On Sunday morning she sees him as the pastor of the church. Can he minister to her? Sometimes. Many pastors and their wives will take time, perhaps one day a week, and go away together. It is their only way of spending time with each other and enjoying one another's company without being interrupted. Just as a wife often cannot pastor a husband, neither can a husband pastor his wife, even if he pastors a church. Though some pastors are extremely skilled counselors, they are often the last to recognize emotional or psychological problems in their own families. When pastors' families need counseling, they will go to a counseling center or a psychologist or another pastor in the area to get the kind of pastoral counsel they need to get. Invariably, hearing the words from someone else makes a difference.

PASTORAL CARE

The congregation, if it would, can pastor a family. It is not enough to shake hands with the pastor at the door on Sunday morning. Befriending the family is just as important. A call to the pastor's wife inviting her to go shopping or an invitation to the family to come for dinner means a lot. The congregation could remember the pastor's wedding anniversary by sending flowers to the home. Marking anniversary dates for number of years serving the church family is a way to let the pastor and his family know that they are appreciated. Another way to show love and affirmation would be to plan a special event, such as a reception or luncheon, for the pastor and his family. That is how pastoral families can be pastored without intruding on their private time together. It is important for them to know they are appreciated. The time *not* to show pastoral care is on Sunday afternoon. Allowing the pastor to rest and to spend time with his family, uninterrupted by calls or visits, is the best form of pastoring a congregation can provide for their pastor.

The congregation doesn't teach the pastor how to love his flock. Instead, pastors teach their congregation to be lovers. As he throws his arms around the congregation each week and preaches and ministers to them, he models Christian love. In a large church, he simply cannot touch every member of the congregation. It is impossible to have a close relationship with everyone once the church reaches five hundred members. This is why the pastoral role of associates is so important. On occasions, like morning worship, he must be loving in such a way that he can touch as many as he can and draw them into himself whether it's shaking hands at the door, visiting briefly with folks at the coffee hour, or hugging the widow who just lost her husband. A physical touch, a personal note of encouragement, and a call to someone in the hospital show love and care. When he does that consistently, throughout his congregation, they can't help but love him in return. It is at this time that the congregation becomes a real community who cares not just for the pastor and his family, but for one another as well.

"Inasmuch as you did it to one of the least of these My brethren, you did it to Me" (Matt. 25:40).

CHAPTER 14

PEOPLE ARE PASTORS, TOO!

"For the equipping of the saints for the work of ministry, for the edifying of the body of Christ."
—Ephesians 4:12

Millions of people sit in the pews on Sunday mornings, worship God, present their tithes and offerings, read the Scriptures daily, have good prayer lives, attend educational classes, and seek to know more of God. They are quietly being equipped to do ministry. Whether it is a ministry in the community, in the marketplace, or in the life of the church, it is still a ministry. We seldom come to that realization on our own.

Week after week we are taught about the Christian life, like a faucet dripping water into a sponge. If we don't squeeze the water out of the sponge, it will become stagnant and sour the sponge. Our churches are full of "sour" Christians who have not been equipped to live out their lives in ministry. Pastors talk at length about an equipping ministry, but they are not always effective at unleashing their members and launching them into service for the Lord. Elton Trueblood said it beautifully: *"We are now a great distance—not only in practice but in theory—from the fellowship of universal witness. Millions are merely backseat Christians, willing to be observers of a performance which the professionals put on, ready to criticize or to applaud, but not willing even to consider the possibility of real participation."* Credentials and ordination are not required to pastor another person. A paraclete is one who comes alongside someone and cares for them. To pastor is to be a paraclete.

It is impossible for pastors of large churches to be beside every member of a congregation, and that is why "equipping the saints for ministry" is so important. The staff of the church should equip the laity to care for and nurture one another in growth. Staff are afraid to do that because they feel that is the pastor's role. The Stephens Ministry (which is so popular in Protestant churches in the United States) and other care-giving ministries are placing a pastoring ministry in the hands of the laity. To pastor a friend requires developing a good listening ear. Sitting quietly with friends while they pour out their souls and helping them to find their own solutions is pastoring. Opening the Scriptures to a friend is pastoring. Praying with a friend is pastoring.

Many laypeople are effective at calling on the sick and visiting shut-ins. During a brief visit they may hold the patient's hand, talk quietly, and pray. That is a pastoral ministry, but laypeople seldom recognize that by doing this they are pastoring someone.

I believe church staffs often fail their congregations by not placing this kind of ministry into the hands of the people. They are not asking the laity to act as pastors, and yet the church lists the ministers as being the entire congregation. It looks nice on the Sunday bulletin, but it is doubtful that the congregation fully realizes what that means. People need to realize that they are called to pastoral ministry through some of the programs and ministries of the church.

In some instances, the support staff members may do more pastoring than pastors do. In receiving a phone call for the pastor, a secretary may give a gentle word of encouragement. If someone comes to the office to see the pastor, the secretary often is the one who calms them and assures them that everything will be all right.

When a church grows large enough to have a number of people on staff, there is a tendency on the part of the congregation to relax and let the staff do it. It has been my experience, especially in affluent churches, to witness the laity pastoring with a checkbook. Having become accustomed to paying for services rendered, church members often write a check to pay for a staff person to do the ministry for them. "Thus also faith by itself, if it does not have works, is dead" (James 2:17). *The Lord wants our heart, then He knows He will have the wallet.*

Two things that immediately come to mind when we talk about service are the mission field and committee work. Most people conclude immediately that the Lord does not want them in Africa or India, so they are not meant for mission work.

Mission awareness begins in the church. There is much that could be done through local outreach to the community, if people would work to resolve it. Instead, what happens? The mission committee tries to staff the committee with everyone who has even a slight interest in mission work. It becomes the biggest committee in the church. Once you are on the mission committee, you are there for life. Meeting faithfully month after month, the committee reads letters from missionaries, listens to people plead for mission money, and takes lengthy minutes. They talk about how the congregation should be more involved in mission but don't take action. If the committee were small, trained, and motivated like a steering committee, more mission and less paper pushing might be accomplished. A small committee could identify mission needs in the community and then recruit members to do mission work rather than talking about doing it.

The work of a committee, in general, can be ministry or misery. More often than we would think, a committee becomes a "holy huddle." A committee is a safe place to meet regularly to discuss the assignment and leave it for staff to implement. Members simply don't have time to do ministry because they have spent vast amounts of time and energy in huge committee meetings. If we would keep our committees small and actively deploy our people in ministry, more would get accomplished for the kingdom. Many concerned, dynamic people refuse to be committee members because they don't want to sit around a table and discuss the same things month after month. They would be involved, however, if they met once or twice, received the task, and were set free from meetings to get the ministry done.

We know we must get exercise to keep our bodies fit,

and so we do what it takes to get in shape. We don't hire someone to jog around the high-school track, expecting that to shape up our sagging figures. It is the same way with lay ministry. Often we spend far too much money staffing ministries that could be done beautifully by the members of the congregation. To change that attitude in the church takes a great deal of motivation. Until that happens, a staff will be paid to do what we could be and should be doing in lay ministry.

The church is a great example of the old story about a football game. There are twenty-two players on the field in need of a rest and thousands of people in the stands in need of exercise. The staff and key leaders do most of the work while everyone else watches.

> *Some people make things happen,*
> *Some people watch things happen,*
> *Some people never know it happened.*

Twenty percent of the people do 80 percent of the work. That is not what the Lord had in mind.

Central Church found itself in a downward spiral when their pastor retired. The members of the church got together and decided they needed to grow in numbers. As the search committee began its process, they decided that to grow in numbers would require an evangelist as the pastor. After all, don't evangelists draw people into the church? They found an evangelist and called him to Central Church. They told him how great Central had been in its heyday and said they were eager for their church to grow to that stature again. But once the pastor began his ministry at Central, the people sat in the pews with their arms crossed and said, "Now, we will watch you make our church grow!"

Church growth comes when the laity become excited about what is going on in the church and share that excitement with others. When we no longer feel comfortable merely warming a pew every week and dropping a check in the offering plate, we will have taken the first step toward ministering to others. There is no greater joy or sense of fulfillment than to actively do Christ's work.

> *Christ has no hands but our*
> *hands to do His work today;*
> *He has no feet but our feet to*
> *lead men in His way;*
> *He has no tongue but our*
> *tongues to tell men how He*
> *died;*
> *He has no help but our help to*
> *bring them to His side.*
> *We are the only Bible the*
> *careless world will read;*
> *We are the sinner's gospel, we*
> *are the scoffer's creed;*
> *We are the Lord's last message*
> *given in deed and word—*
> *What if the line is crooked?*
> *What if the type is blurred?*
> *What if our hands are busy*
> *with other work than His?*
> *What if our feet are walking*
> *where sin's allurement is?*
> *What if our tongues are*

*speaking of things His lips
would spurn?
How can we hope to help Him
unless from Him we learn?*

—Annie Johnson Flint

CHAPTER 15

VULNERABLE TO ATTACK

◆

"Be sober, be vigilant; because your adversary the devil walks about like a roaring lion, seeking whom he may devour. Resist him, steadfast in the faith."
                                              —1 Peter 5:8

One of the greatest strategies of our enemy is to divide and conquer. From the beginning of creation, Satan has attempted to separate us from God and from each other.

Jesus teaches us to live in unity and to be likeminded with Him and each other. That is one of the great challenges we face when we follow Jesus Christ as Lord.

The church comprises persons who are diverse in age, intelligence, talents, and skills, and with all that diversity, God asks us to live in unity and be likeminded!

When a church has ceased growing, has become apathetic, and is content with itself, Satan has succeeded one more time. He knows that if he attempted to destroy a church all at once, the church would rise up and gain great strength. His strategy, then, is to slowly immobilize it. He knows that if he can move it into complacent Christianity it will not take any strident steps forward. If a church has moved to a maintenance ministry, it will only be a matter of time when Satan claims a victory.

When a church is active, alive, growing, and moving forward, Satan knows how to stir up conflict, anxiety, and tension, especially among the staff and leadership. Satan is so subtle in his ways that when he moves stumbling blocks into our way, we fail to recognize his craftiness. We view those blocks as minor interruptions, frustrations, or disappointments. Seldom do we recognize a spiritual attack in its early stages. Instead we continue to try to do the work, but the tyranny of the urgent slows us down and drains our energy. One thing after another deters our progress. As the pressure and frustration build, conflict management moves into high gear. Satan is having a heyday! In the last five years, as I have visited churches all over our country, I have become more and more aware of the evil and oppressive forces that are in the world. At first I didn't understand it, but after witnessing it being repeated in many churches, I became aware of what Satan does. I work to help a church function more effectively in their ministry. That usually means opening up some bottlenecks that have occurred. Sometimes that involves a study of the staff and committee structure; sometimes it involves evaluating program, communication, and other elements that comprise the total ministry of the church. As I work with the staff and leaders of the congregation, we explore ways of building better and stronger ministry. When they begin to implement the plans some wonderful things begin to happen in their church.

Spiritual attacks come from where you would least expect it. I have often seen churches come under attack immediately after my visit. Pastors become ill, key staff people leave the church under unusual circumstances, conflict rises from very unexpected sources, crisis events occur that will consume staff energy, a trusted friend betrays the pastor for no apparent reason. Conflict in the staff over a simple issue causes turmoil for weeks or months. These are just a few of the signs of attack.

In one situation, the pastor was extremely ill with the flu and never got out of bed the entire week of my visit. Because he was so ill, I could not spend any time at all with him and had to work without his guidance. I found in that church an oppressiveness that drained my energy to the point of weakness each day. The office I was using seemed dark and hollow. It was difficult to communicate with the people as they came to talk with me. It felt cold, and the heaviness was difficult for me to shake off. Normally it is not unusual for me to work fourteen hours day after day. Not so with this church. At the end of seven or eight hours, I was so exhausted I could barely walk out of the building. By the third or fourth day, I began to realize that this was, indeed, an attack of Satan. I began to investigate the history of the church and found some unhealthy things in the life of the church that went back thirty-five years.

Eight years before, the pastor at that time had carried on numerous affairs with women in the congregation. I discovered that the office I was using and other places in the church were the settings for many of his amorous adventures. This explained why I discerned what I did as I walked through various areas of the church buildings. Though the pastor had been removed from the church, the evil remained.

A young pastor had been called to the church, and though some ministry was accomplished, within three or four years he took a call to another church. In talking with him about his ministry in this troubled church, he said he felt like he was preaching into the wind. He felt his energy completely drained from him each day and that he eventually did most of his work from his home where it was safe.

There was no question in my mind why the present pastor was as sick as he was. Satan was doing all he could to prevent that church from breaking out of apathy and moving into a vital ministry for the Lord.

Unfortunately no one recognized the oppressive force of Satan and how it was affecting the church. What had happened in the past was, to them, an unfortunate set of circumstances. However, a few people who had been very good friends with the former pastor continued to hold significant positions in the church. Though the pastor had been removed from the pulpit, he lived nearby and associated with these church members. His negative influence continued to be felt through these people and the evil atmosphere remained. Almost everyone in this troubled congregation was unaware of the evil hold on the church.

The best of times can be the worst of times. When a church becomes excited about building new ministry, the struggle they encounter can be almost unbearable.

As I prepare to leave a church after a consultation, I discuss spiritual warfare with the pastor and encourage him to put on the full armor of God each day. I tell him to watch for the attack and be ready for it. Regularly the pastor calls a week or so after my visit to thank me for the warning and explain what happened. Each story is different.

We all hear stories about difficult or troubled churches, but seldom does anyone take the time to peel away the layers of the church to find the core of the difficulty. In the beginning, *a spiritual attack can be so insignificant that it is not recognizable.* Like a cancer, it takes root and grows long before a person experiences any discomfort or pain. Churches can go for years with one minor thing after another gradually slowing down ministry and spiritual growth.

Then one day the church treasurer is discovered embezzling funds, or word surfaces that a pastor has been seducing the women of the church, or a faction in the congregation is motivating people to leave the church. Suddenly what was under the surface has become a full-blown barrage, and ministry can come to a screeching halt. We work to resolve the present crisis and then go on about ministry, never taking the time to get to the core of the problem and eliminate it. And so a year or two will go by and the church will be somewhat recovered and something major will happen again. Until someone gets to the core, it will continue to take the church down.

Satan is effective at hitting at the self-image of a congregation. Over time a congregation will come to believe that they are a bunch of losers and that they will never be healthy again. Depending on the problems, a team of people with the gift of discernment may have to spend significant time investigating the history of the problems and then determine the course of action.

Jack Hayford wrote in his book, *Rebuilding the Real You,* "The essential need for recognizing the work of the devil through demonic devices is that the defeat of any adversary must begin by identifying him and discerning his methods of operation. Discernment can make the difference between fighting the enemy or condemning yourself."

FIT FOR BATTLE

Many destructive things that often seem unexplainable are from an influence that is not of God. By being aware of those forces, the pastor, staff, and congregation can battle them and claim victory. The Bible provides the battle plan and all the necessary equipment. The strategy for encountering the enemy and claiming victory is found in Ephesians 6:10–18.

Finally, my brethren, be strong in the Lord and in the power of His might. Put on the whole armor of God, that you may be able to stand against the wiles of the devil. For we do not wrestle against flesh and blood, but against principalities, against powers, against the rulers of the darkness of this age, against spiritual hosts of wickedness in the heavenly places. Therefore take up the whole armor of God, that you may be able to withstand in the evil day, and having done all, to stand. Stand therefore, having girded your waist with truth, having put on the breastplate of righteousness, and having shod your feet with the preparation of the gospel of peace; above all, taking the shield of faith with which you will be able to quench all the fiery darts of the wicked one. And take the helmet of salvation, and the sword of the Spirit, which is the word of God; praying always with all prayer and supplication in the Spirit, being watchful to this end with all perseverance and supplication for all the saints.

Be strong in the Lord and in the power of His might. The key is recognizing a spiritual attack in its early stages and trusting in the power of God to put down the evil forces.

Put on the whole armor of God, that you may be able to stand against the wiles of the devil. Often we attempt to do battle half-prepared. No soldier goes into battle without being fully dressed for it.

Our struggle is not against flesh and blood, but against the powers of the dark world and the spiritual forces of evil in the heavenly realms. Paul draws the battle lines in this passage and warns us that we are battling an unseen enemy; we will experience the work of his hand but will not see him.

Therefore take up the whole armor of God, that you may be able to withstand in the evil day. This is our first order for battle. Earlier God told us to be equipped; now He tells us to prepare for the attack.

And having done all, to stand. Stand therefore. Three times God has told us to stand our ground. It is clear we are to hold the line, not ignore the situation. We must not turn our back on it nor run from it, but stand, and stand strong.

Having girded your waist with truth. Time for an equipment check. Truth is a major weapon against Satan. There is no way to negotiate with him, for he is the chief of liars. Anything less than the truth gives him the edge. It is important to get to the core of the problem. When we do, we find the truth.

Having put on the breastplate of righteousness. This piece of equipment protects our torso, especially our heart. Just as the breastplate protected the Roman soldier from swords and spears, the breastplate of righteousness will protect us from the "fiery darts of the evil one." Righteousness, simply put, is doing right when we know we should. Doing the right thing is not always the popular action to take, but we have not been called to be popular.

And having shod your feet with the preparation of the gospel of peace. Boots for battle are not delicate little sandals, or shiny new loafers. These boots give our feet support and protection. They allow us to be steady on our feet, and insatiable when the blows come. When we lace up the boots, we have laced the peace of God around ourselves. In following God's lead, we can march stalwartly into battle.

Above all, taking the shield of faith with which you will be able to quench all the fiery darts of the wicked one. We are taught that faith comes by hearing the Word of God. The shield of faith is our daily study of the Scriptures. Through our study the Holy Spirit prepares us and arms us for whatever the battle will bring.

Take the helmet of salvation. . . . The helmet of salvation is what protects us against evil-inspired thoughts, and ideas that flash before our mind's eye. Without this protection we can be bombarded with fears, lust, pride, and doubts that can deter us in the battle being waged. We must wear our helmet at all times.

The sword of the Spirit, which is the word of God;

praying always with all prayer and supplication in the Spirit. The shield of faith comes by hearing the Word of God. The sword of the Spirit is the Word of God. The shield is our defense, the sword is our offense. Now, standing firm with the sword in hand, we are ready for the battle. The orders to the "front lines" come through prayer. Prolonged seasons of prayer may be very helpful, especially by those who are standing in support and not on the front lines of battle. However, in the midst of great spiritual struggle, the Holy Spirit will provide insights and answers to our prayers. We must respond to those answers. The Holy Spirit brings principles or promises from the Scripture to our minds that apply to our struggle, and that is a thrust of the sword of the Spirit.

Jesus retaliated against Satan many times. In the heat of battle, just repeating the name of Jesus will often bring the release of the power needed to claim a victory. God's promises as recorded in the Scriptures and our prayers led by the Holy Spirit are more than Satan can handle. Continued prayer will retrieve what he has captured; when this is accomplished, the victory belongs to God.

> *And though this world with devils filled,*
> *Should threaten to undo us,*
> *We will not fear, for God has willed,*
> *His truth to triumph through us.*
> *The prince of darkness grim,*
> *We tremble not for him,*
> *His rage we can endure,*
> *For lo, his doom is sure;*
> *One little word shall fell him.*
> *That word above all earthly powers,*

No thanks to them abideth;
The Spirit and the gifts are ours,
Through Him who with us sideth.
Let goods and kindred go,
This mortal life also,
The body they may kill;
God's truth abideth still;
His kingdom is forever.

"Unless there is within us, that which is above us, we will soon yield to that which is around us!"

CHAPTER 16

BROKEN TO BE WHOLE

"I sought the Lord, and afterward I knew
He moved my soul to seek Him, seeking
  me;
It was not I that found, O Savior true,
No, I was found of thee."
                              —*Unknown*

"My greatest humiliation was the beginning
of God's greatest use of my life. He chose the
one experience in which I could not glory, for
His glory."
                              —*Charles Colson*

A beautiful young woman came to me to discuss
one of the committees of the church with whom she
was involved. After discussing her concerns I commented that this was something to make a matter of
prayer. The words were barely off my lips when she
dissolved into tears. I quickly comforted her and asked

what I had done to cause this to happen. Collecting herself, she said, "You asked me to pray, and that is the problem! I struggle so with praying to a heavenly Father, when my own father abused me for so many years throughout my childhood and into adolescence."

The newspapers are full of dramatic accounts of child abuse. The nightly news graphically illustrates man's inhumanity to man. Rape and incest are common topics in the media. The scars of abuse are heavy burdens for a person to carry throughout a lifetime. Though we may repress those painful memories, our past experiences affect who we are and who we will be in the future. It is only in recent years that people have gained the courage to talk about the things that have happened to them in the past. Today, rape victims report the crime to authorities when years ago they were too embarrassed to tell anyone. Teachers who recognize that a child has been molested file a report and the abuse is investigated. Battered women and children have come out of hiding and are seeking help. Counseling centers have been established to work with victims of abuse to help them overcome the pain so that they can live the kind of life God intends for them. We hear regularly about drug abuse, alcohol abuse, and child abuse. The steady stream of people who visit counselors are struggling to cope with problems of living in the '90s. For many, the struggle began with abusive behavior in their earlier years like the beautiful young woman who came to me.

These are dramatic cases, and most of us have not experienced those circumstances. However, there is a far more subtle form of abuse that often does just as much harm. Verbal abuse at an early age can destroy a child's sense of self-worth and wound his tender spirit in many ways. Constant criticism by a sibling takes its toll on a person's life and personality. Though verbal and physical abuse may be easily found in unhappy homes or in parents with addictive behaviors, it can also be found in a home that appears to be happy and secure.

Without ever being aware it is happening, many people have been abused. They have thought that they grew up in a very healthy home, only to learn later in life that they were treated terribly. That abuse, though it may not have left visible scars on their bodies, has left deep scars on their souls. As adults they find that some of the abusive things that happened to them as a child are being evidenced in the way they think, act, respond, and live.

Goal-oriented parents who continually push their children to turn "B" work into an "A" are striking blows to a child's spirit. Parents who show favoritism of one child over another diminish the second child's self-worth. Parents or family members who constantly tell a child that he is not good enough, that he can't measure up, or that he is stupid wound that child emotionally. Negative comments that are not countered with expressions of love and affirmation wound a child's tender spirit. Often this is hidden, but when the child becomes an adult the wounds manifest themselves in rejection, obsessive-compulsive behavior, possessiveness, perfectionism, low self-worth, and other abnormalities.

The first step toward healing is for a person to recognize he has been wounded and become open to being helped. Often we visit a counselor or pastor with a problem that is only a symptom of the real issue. Trusting a pastor or counselor plays a big part in the eventual healing of the person.

Great portions of a pastor's life are spent counseling people. A pastor will spend hours listening to someone unfold painful events in his past. Then as gently and lovingly as possible, a pastor helps put his life back together. Pastors are discovering today that the basic psychology courses in seminary are not enough to handle some of the complex situations that are presented to them. Subsequent training, sometimes on the master's or doctoral level, provides them the counseling techniques necessary to help even the most troubled.

Pastors must be extremely careful not to become emotionally involved with the people they counsel. Often pastors allow themselves to be caught up in the concerns of the counselee. One thing leads to another, they become romantically involved, and what began as a sincere act of care and compassion becomes destructive to both people.

Pastors become depressed, discouraged, and fatigued when they carry the burdens of a counselee. They must always keep in mind that they are to be the conduit for the healing power of God to flow through to the counselee. Though a counseling experience may drain energy from the person seeking counsel, it also drains a lot from the counselor. If the counselor attempts this on his own energy and not on God's power, the fatigue will be extremely difficult to overcome.

When a pastor takes a few minutes prior to the session to relax and focus on God, he opens the conduit for God's energy to flow. Following the session, if he follows the same pattern, he releases the burden to God and is set free from the weight of the previous hour.

If the pastor does not guard his calendar, he could spend his entire week counseling people. Recognizing the tremendous need for this type of care, many churches have hired professional counselors to relieve the counseling load on the pastor. In some situations, the church has established a counseling center that provides lay listeners, support groups, licensed counselors, and psychologists. Many pastors will counsel a person three times. If they see it will take more than those visits to help the person, they will refer the person to a counselor who can help them for an extended period. Some churches even help pay for some of the counseling when the pastor makes these referrals. This has been a relief to a very busy pastor.

HEALING OF MEMORIES

Years ago, Agnes Sanford wrote of God's power to heal not only our physical infirmities but our crippled emotions as well. More recently, Francis MacNutt, David Seamands, and many others have written extensively about the ministry of inner healing, the healing of memories. Their books have taught pastors and counselors how to recognize the wounds that people carry, and how to seek God's power to heal them. The ministry of inner healing, is alive and well in churches today.

Recognizing that people are talking more openly today about the pain they have experienced in the past, the ministry of inner healing is being used more and more as a tool to help the victims of abuse.

Pastors, counselors, and laypersons with keen insight are becoming equipped to work with people in inner healing. The pastor, counselor, or layperson then can lead the people to a place where they can visualize Jesus in the setting where they were so wounded and can allow Him to heal their wounds. When they are open to receiving that healing touch in their life and someone is equipped to lead them through the experience, they can be set free.

As I work with pastors, I often find that many of them have been abused. Some have sought counsel, dealt with the problems, and gained victory. Others have experienced abuse in such subtle ways that they don't recognize it has affected their self-image and how they minister and interact with people. Perhaps the reason for a pastor's drivenness, rebellion to form and structure, workaholic nature, or resistance to authority can be explained by looking to his past.

It is not unusual to find pastors who have had a difficult relationship with their father or mother. How do they cope with that and resolve it? *The answer is that we have a great God who was, is, and always will be a healer.* As surely as He is present with us today, He was present with us in our formative years. Pastors who extend a healing ministry to their members may be in desperate need of healing themselves. They have not been raised free of scars, and they struggle with many of the same issues that they counsel others about. To whom do they turn for help? Christ fills the void once occupied by the wound and life takes on new meaning. Along with the healing comes renewed verve, energy, and freedom that allow ministry to become deeper and more meaningful than ever.

When we become physically ill, we identify the symptoms and get medical help. Seldom do we recognize emotional illness and seek out a counselor. Even though we may come to a crisis time in our lives and decide we need counseling, we rarely know the true reason we are in crisis. A trained pastor or counselor can probe into the depths of our pain.

Pastors, like everyone else, have deep wounds that

need to be healed. The nature of their career is such that they are more care-giving than care-receiving. They don't recognize their wounds, and so they don't seek counsel. If a staff person identifies some problem areas, rarely will he share that information with the pastor. If a pastor is to be helped, he must first face the fact that he has a problem and then find someone he can trust to help him. Seldom will a pastor seek a colleague in ministry. He doesn't want to appear weak, and he is fearful that word will leak out that he has problems.

Bill had invited me to conduct an overview of his church ministry. The work was progressing very nicely, and we were building a good relationship. During the late evening hours, we would reflect upon the events of the day and talk about ministry—his and mine. One evening he asked me some questions that uncorked pain, frustration, and anger that I had repressed for years. He helped me to see that it was affecting my sense of self-worth as well as my ministry.

Refusing to admit to myself that I needed counseling, I allowed Bill to "nurture" me as a friend. Long after my work at his church was completed, Bill and I kept working on me.

It was during this time that he introduced me to the ministry of inner healing and convinced me that Christ could heal my broken self-worth.

We did not know what the Lord would do. All I knew was that I trusted my friend to lead me to the face of Jesus. That evening transformed my life, and healed the broken pieces I had carried around for so long.

I was grateful to Bill for the time he invested in me, for his caring spirit, and for the way he reached out to me. In return I told him that I would like to be that person for him one day if the need arose.

As time passed, the Lord showed me that I should help others with inner healing. So Bill became my tutor. He outlined a course of study, we discussed counseling situations, and I sat with him as he led others to Christ for healing, just as he did for me.

Through the many long days and months of working together, the bond of trust and friendship grew stronger. Bill shared with me some of his background and the wounds he received as a boy. Slowly and painfully he recognized that he had been harboring some fears deep within himself that needed God's healing touch. For healing to take place, it meant Bill would have to be willing to give up control of this part of his life. Bill would have to surrender to the healing power of Jesus Christ.

After great struggle he decided to risk everything, and he asked me to walk through a time of inner healing with him. This was my final exam in inner healing, and he warned me not to mess it up.

Late one Sunday afternoon, the two of us went to his church and made our way to the chancel steps of the sanctuary. We made our hearts still before the Lord and prayed for protection from any evil force that would interrupt or interfere with God's healing. Then we began the long and painful process of seeking inner healing of his painful memories.

In time my friend began to confess his deep-seated fear that had been with him since he was a small boy. He had reached a place of brokenness and surrender. Weary of carrying this fear, he had come to the end of his rope; Christ was there to carry his burden. It was a heart-rending experience to be a paraclete for my friend as he slowly and painfully surrendered his fear to Christ. God gently and lovingly removed his fear, giving Bill complete assurance that it was no longer his problem. Then He poured the power of the Holy Spirit in the void and bound the wound with His love and assurance.

That afternoon Bill took a significant step in surrendering pain from his past. It took time for the healing to be completed. But when the old fear reappeared Bill would remember the picture Christ gave him of relief and peace and the fear would fade.

Having dealt with this aspect of his life, darts that once went straight to the core of his fear now are deflected and carry no pain.

Bill's ministry has grown stronger as a result of inner healing. In time, he may seek healing for other hurts as well. What caused Bill to take this step? The Holy Spirit kept prompting Bill to relinquish control over this area of his life.

When we experience inner healing, our senses become more sharply attuned to the needs of those around us. We become aware of others around us who have similar wounds. The capacity to empathize and sympathize with someone as they share their pain is heightened. We know that there is a way out of the painful darkness of the past, and we can extend hope to those who hurt.

There is hope today for healing the wounds of our past, but we must be willing to let Christ do the healing.

ABUSE IN THE CHURCH

Silent abuse runs rampant throughout the church. I am constantly amazed at how Christians treat one another. One pastor told me that an elder sat on his board for six years and never opened his mouth during a meeting, but talked openly about the pastor behind his back. That's abuse!

Another pastor knew that some people in his congregation were not happy with him or his style of ministry. None would talk with the pastor about it; they just wanted him to leave the church. They withheld their giving to the operating budget but continued to give to missions and special projects in the church. One individual partly subsidized a missions trip for the pastor and his wife but continued to tell his friends and other staff members of his displeasure with the pastor. Yet he never confronted him personally. That's abuse!

Personnel committees are notorious for accumulating negative information about a pastor and never sharing it with him in order to help him to improve. They will, instead, hold it in reserve and use it when they want to move the pastor out of the church. That's abuse!

These are just a few illustrations of the kind of abuse pastors receive. If they are not carrying any deep wounds from the past, it stings for a while, and they keep moving forward. But if they struggle with rejection or perfectionism, the information doesn't sting, it wounds. It goes deep into their soul, can cause sleepless nights, and shatters their self-confidence. It can be devastating.

During these times a pastor may come to grips with the fact that he needs help in understanding his pain. This might be the moment when he will become vulnerable enough to seek help from a counselor who can see beyond the present hurt and into the wounds received years earlier.

For so many of us, it takes being broken before we

can be made whole. The process is certainly painful. But those who have surrendered their broken state to Christ rejoice in the healing and wholeness present in their life. They sing with David: "Bless the LORD, O my soul; And all that is within me, bless His holy name! Bless the LORD, O my soul, And forget not all His benefits: Who forgives all your iniquities, Who heals all your diseases, Who redeems your life from destruction, Who crowns you with lovingkindness and tender mercies, Who satisfies your mouth with good things, So that your youth is renewed like the eagle's" (Ps. 103:1–5).

CHAPTER 17

A HEART FOR GOD AND A GOD FOR ALL HEARTS

"Then I will give them a heart to know Me, that I am the LORD; and they shall be My people, and I will be their God, for they shall return to Me with their whole heart."

—*Jeremiah 24:7*

"Either Christ is Lord of all, or not Lord at all."

—*Lloyd Ogilvie*

A great portion of this book has focused on pastors, staff, committees, and the inner workings of the church. I have attempted to explain how pastors transmit all of what they are about, and how and why they receive all of what the parish is about. I cannot close this book, however, without adding the final element that makes the church the family of God. That element is how the members of the congregation receive what is being transmitted and how they transmit that information to others. All too often, the garbled communication is not in the transmitter but in the receiver. It is not always the flaws of the pastor but of the people who are not receptive.

We learn from pastors, preachers, teachers, and communicators. If we are not transmitting to others what we have received, there is definitely something wrong. We cannot lead someone farther than where we are ourselves. If we have not incorporated what we are being taught, we certainly cannot effectively communicate it to others. We must ask ourselves:

"Do I know who I am?"

"Do I know where I am going?"

"Do I know what God has called me to do?"

These are the key questions to unlocking what life holds for us. To find the answers we must surrender ourselves to the Lord. As He reveals Himself to us, we discover life anew for ourselves.

Years of sitting in the pew and attending Bible classes, conferences, and retreats have given the layperson what I call "pew-gained theology." Our theology has been learned in the church rather than in the seminary, and from the Scriptures and a few good books, rather than from theologians. *Pew-gained theology*. What is it? It is "the study of religious faith, practice, and experience acquired through consistent attendance to hearing the Word of God preached and taught, through independent study, translating what is learned to practical daily living, and reproducing that pattern in others." It is that ability to communicate to others in practical, everyday terms the width, breadth, height, and depth of Christianity.

Some of us are slow learners, and it takes years to understand our faith enough to communicate it to others. Some people are exceptional students but find studying more fascinating than sharing the good news with others. And then there are those who hold forth a winsome witness to all, friend and stranger alike.

Have you noticed that when you are with someone for a while you pick up that person's mannerisms or expressions? You may adopt your friend's slang, vocabulary, and accent. A secretary will often be able to finish a sentence her boss begins, because she knows him well enough to know his mind. After listening to the same pastor for a period of time, do we find ourselves incorporating into our language significant phrases, Scripture verses, and illustrations that have come from his preaching? The steady communication of the "mind of Christ" reaches out from the heart of the pastor to the hearts of the people. The pastor, with a true heart for God, shares with us in the pew a God for all hearts. As we incorporate that steady communication into our hearts and souls, slowly our heart is molded by the tender hand of God and it becomes a heart for God. That is only the first step in building the church, the family of God. It is up to us, with our "pew-gained theology," to share with others the God for all hearts.

Christianity is one generation away from extinction. We must become reproducible Christians, extending our faith to others. We must be willing and ready to step out in faith. As we take that important step and reach out to others, the Sunday worship experience will take on new meaning. Instead of coming to church "to get something that will carry us for the week," we will come to worship God on Sunday morning and praise Him for the great things He has accomplished in the past week. The words of the pastor will ring in our hearts in a new way. The preaching of the Word will take on new meaning. Familiar phrases, thought patterns, and illustrations become tools for our witness. The message of the hour will be so graphic, we will find ourselves saying, "Yes, that happened to me this week. That's exactly what I thought or said or did." The sermon will no longer be a one-way message; it will be one we will participate in as we receive it and apply it where it best fits. Sunday morning will become a time of celebration, rejoicing, and praising God. Christianity is meant to be contagious.

"That might happen if you have a super, dynamic preacher," some people will say. I say it will happen in every church, regardless of the charisma or delivery of the preacher, if the gospel is presented and the people in the pew surrender their hearts to God. *Denominations may come and go, but God's kingdom on earth will continue to grow. It will grow through the faithful preaching of the Word and by hearing His voice and obeying His Will.*

Pastors in tall steeples or in country churches are not the only eagles. Eagles are everywhere: in the boardroom, at the kitchen sink, at the drawing board, in an operating room, in a mine shaft, in the fields, in the cockpit, in every walk of life. We are the ones He has called, chosen, elected, and ordained to do His work.

The distance between pulpit and pew may be twenty or thirty feet. The distance between pastor and parishioner can be greater still if there is not a conscious awareness that we are all equal in the sight of God. It is the communion table, often placed between the pulpit and the pew, that is the common denominator that draws to it all who claim the name of Christ.

When we come to the table, pastor and people, we come as pilgrims on a journey of faith needing to be ministered to by the Holy Spirit. All of us, with our successes and failures, joys and sorrows, come before God to confess our sins and receive His forgiveness. Around that table are pilgrims called together to be the company of the committed for Jesus Christ, each one with different tasks to accomplish for Him. For when we meet Him in eternity, it will not matter how many Sundays someone waxed eloquent in the pulpit, or how many anthems we sang in the choir, or how many children we taught in Sunday school, or how many homeless we fed. What will matter is that what we did in life was done with a servant's spirit and was motivated by a heart for Him, and that we loved others because He loved us first. A heart for God, reaching up to Him; a God for all hearts, reaching out to others. To everyone who names the name of Jesus, as Lord of their life, my hope is that you will be what God intends for you to be.

> *To be the family of God,*
> *Not just a congregation filling pews,*
> *That you would love one another.*
> *To be students of the Scripture,*
> *Not just Bible carriers,*
> *That you would know the mind of God.*
> *To be forgiving of others,*
> *Not just condescending or accepting,*

That you might experience the true forgiveness of
    Christ.
To be set free by the power of the Holy Spirit,
    Not just content to be a half-filled Christian,
    That you might know the awesome adventure of
        serving Him.
To be participants for God, equipped for ministry,
    Not just onlookers,
    That you might rediscover who you are.
To be a winsome witness for Jesus Christ,
    Not just a quiet observer of the faith,
    That you would bear much fruit.
To be involved in the local church with heart, soul,
    mind, and wallet,
    Not just the person in the pew,
    That you would make the difference for Eternity.
To be a lover of God,
    Not just another religious person,
    That you might sense His touch.
    And know His complete and abundant love,
To have a heart for God,
    Not just your mind or intellect,
    That you would share a God for all hearts.

"Now you are the body of Christ, and members individually" (1 Cor. 12:27).

THE CHRISTIAN

The Christian
Is born-again.
Can be found throughout the world.
Comes in many shapes and sizes.
Looks courageous and proud, but may be timid on
  the inside.
Has keen insight.
Sees things from God's perspective.
Is a visionary.
Experiences total freedom when surrendered to
  Christ.
Is set apart by God.
Knows his territory.
Is a lone witness of Christ.
Gathers with other Christians for fellowship.
Trusts his future to God.

   "Yet I will not forget you. See, I have inscribed you
on the palms of My hands" (Isa. 49:14b–15a).